Books and
Articles on
South Carolina History

LEWIS P. JONES is head of the history department at Wofford College, South Carolina.

Books and Articles on South Carolina History

A List for Laymen

Lewis P. Jones

TRICENTENNIAL BOOKLET NUMBER **8**

Published for the South Carolina Tricentennial Commission
by the University of South Carolina Press
Columbia, South Carolina

iv

Preface

More than most types, booklets such as this, which are designed simply as tools, need to have their purpose clearly set forth. The basic aim of this guide is to suggest titles from among which intelligent readers (not necessarily academicians) by their own trials and errors ought to be able to find enough good reading to satisfy some of their interests in South Carolina history or even to conduct their own "teach-yourself-history" course.

In describing the nature of the booklet, the compiler finds it easiest to say what it is not. (1) It is not a historiography —an essay on historians, schools of historical thought, or various historical interpretations. (2) It is not a listing of book condensations or even book reviews. (3) It is not a bibliography. But it does have some features of all of these, as it is an incomplete, selected bibliography (for readers but not researchers), with some annotations about a few of the major writings (designed to lure some readers to test certain books while tipping off others that these definitely would not be of special interest to them), and some of these annotations perhaps convey a very slight historiography.

Hopefully, two features may enhance its usefulness. The items listed are generally available—if not always in print and in book stores, at least in reasonably good public libraries and college libraries. Second, it includes articles in periodicals which contain so much useful writing on South Carolina history—where it is too often neglected, unnoticed, and not indexed.

Readers should be aware, however, of excellent and full bibliographies which do exist. Especially good is J. Harold Easterby: *Guide to the Study and Reading of South Caro-*

Organization of Booklet

Anyone seeking to use this booklet must be aware of its organization if it is to serve its purpose. The chapters are basically chronological. Each is devoted to one rather arbitrarily selected period of history.

Within each chapter, the suggested readings are divided into the following categories:

A. SPECIAL STUDIES which concentrate on the specified period of South Carolina history.

B. GENERAL STUDIES IN SOUTHERN AND AMERICAN HISTORY, usually those which stress that particular period and which include useful sections on the South Carolina aspect of the story.

C. GENERAL HISTORIES OF SOUTH CAROLINA, "the standard studies," with an indication of the chapters or pages pertinent to the period covered by the chapter.

D. SPECIAL TOPICS. Books and articles dealing with specific issues, persons, and topics of the period. Much of the social history will be found in this section, which will emphasize magazine articles.

E. CONTEMPORARY DESCRIPTIONS, the eyewitness record of the different periods as found in diaries, memoirs, and travelers' accounts.

F. OLD ACCOUNTS BY EARLY HISTORIANS, now long outdated and written usually before the day of the "scientifically trained historian." These have their limitations, but they also have their uses and some readers like them. Most of these deal with the Colonial and Revolutionary periods. Many have recently been reprinted.

Note on Publication
and Bibliographical Data

Normally, bibliographical data about a publication will be given the *first* time it is listed but *not* thereafter. No effort has been made to indicate whether titles are currently in print, but those that are scarce and that have long been out of print generally have been omitted. This does not mean that everything herein is in every county library, but accessibility has been a major guideline in selection. For example, almost all of the venerated old historians included are those which have been reprinted in the last two decades.

Place of publication is indicated for original editions which have long been out of print and are probably not easily obtainable. The name of the press is listed for more recent publications and for reprints. If a paperback edition appeared, its publisher is also listed; if no publisher of the paperback is listed, the publisher is the same as given for the hardback edition.

Abbreviations

Amer. Hist. Assoc., *Annual Report*. The *Annual Report* of the American Historical Association.

Amer. Hist. Rev.: American Historical Review.

Columbia U Press: Columbia University Press, New York, N. Y.

Duke U Press: Duke University Press, Durham, N. C.

Ga. Hist. Qtrly.: Georgia Historical Quarterly.

Ga. Rev.: Georgia Review.

Harvard U Press: Harvard University Press, Cambridge, Mass.

Jour. Negro Hist.: Journal of Negro History.

Jour. Sou. Hist.: Journal of Southern History.

LSU Press: Louisiana State University Press, Baton Rouge, La.

Memphis St Coll Press: Memphis State College Press, Memphis, Tenn.

Negro U Press: Negro Universities Press (A Division of Greenwood Publishing Corporation).

N. C. Hist. Rev.: North Carolina Historical Review.

Ohio State U Press: Ohio State University Press, Columbus, Ohio.

Oxford U Press: Oxford University Press, New York, N. Y.

So. Atl. Qtrly.: South Atlantic Quarterly.

S. C. Hist. Assoc. *Procdgs.:* South Carolina Historical Association *Proceedings.*

S. C. Hist. Mag.: *South Carolina Historical Magazine* (in its earlier years, published as *South Carolina Historical and Genealogical Magazine*).

S. C. Hist. Soc. *Collections:* South Carolina Historical Society

Collections. (These were collections of papers gathered and published at irregular intervals by the Society which now publishes the *South Carolina Historical Magazine.*)

S. C. Hist. Illus.: South Carolina History Illustrated.

Stanford U Press: Stanford University Press, Stanford, Calif.

U of Ala Press: University of Alabama Press, University, Ala.

U of Chi Press: University of Chicago Press, Chicago, Ill.

U of Fla Press: University of Florida Press, Gainesville, Fla.

U of Ga Press: University of Georgia Press, Athens, Ga.

U of Mich Press: University of Michigan Press, Ann Arbor, Mich.

U of N Mex Press: University of New Mexico Press, Albuquerque, N. Mex.

U of NC Press: University of North Carolina Press, Chapel Hill, N. C.

U of Okla Press: University of Oklahoma Press, Norman, Okla.

U of Pa Press: University of Pennsylvania Press, Philadelphia, Pa.

U of SC Press: University of South Carolina Press, Columbia, S. C.

U of Tenn Press: University of Tennessee Press, Knoxville, Tenn.

U. S. Pubs: United States Publishers Association.

Va. Qtrly Rev.: Virginia Quarterly Review.

Wm. & Mary Qtrly.: William and Mary Quarterly.

Yale U Press: Yale University Press, New Haven, Conn.

Introduction

Thus far, there has been no major cooperative general series on South Carolina history—no multivolume work issued by one publisher, with a general editor and a number of authors, each a specialist in his field who produces a volume about one particular period. There is nothing like the *American Nation* series, issued by Harper's, or the ten-volume *History of the South,* now being completed by the LSU Press.

Nevertheless, if one wanted to read or to assemble such a series for South Carolina, he should have access to or acquire the following books (herein listed chronologically by the periods which they cover). They are usually recognized by scholars as the more useful monographs on these periods; their emphasis is on political history.

1. Edward McCrady, *History of South Carolina Under the Proprietary Government, 1670–1719* (Macmillan, 1897; Reprints: Russell, 1969; AMS Press, 1969).

2. M. Eugene Sirmans, *Colonial South Carolina: A Political History, 1663–1763* (U of NC Press, 1966).

3. Verner Crane, *Southern Frontier, 1670–1733* (Duke U Press, 1929; Paperback: U of Mich Press, 1956).

4. Robert L. Meriwether, *Expansion of South Carolina, 1729–1765* (Kingsport: Southern Publishers, 1940).

5. Edward McCrady, *History of South Carolina Under the Royal Government, 1719–1775* (Macmillan, 1899; Reprint: Russell, 1969; AMS Press, 1969).

6. John R. Alden, *The Revolution in the South, 1763–1789* (LSU Press, 1957).

1

7. J. Harold Wolfe, *Jeffersonian Democracy in South Carolina* (U of NC Press, 1940; also, Paperback).

8. William W. Freehling, *Prelude to Civil War: The Nullification Controversy in South Carolina, 1816–1836* (Harper & Row, 1966; Paperback: Harper Torchbooks).

9. Philip M. Hamer, *Secession Movement in South Carolina, 1847–1852* (Allentown, Pa.: Haas & Co., 1918).

10. Henry S. Schultz, *Nationalism and Sectionalism in South Carolina, 1852–1860* (Duke U Press, 1950; Reprint: Da Capo Press, 1969).

11. Charles E. Cauthen, *South Carolina Goes to War, 1860–1865* (U of NC Press, 1950).

12. Joel Williamson, *After Slavery: The Negro in South Carolina During Reconstruction, 1861–1877* (U of NC Press, 1965; Paperback, 1969).

13. Francis B. Simkins and Robert H. Woody, *South Carolina During Reconstruction* (U of NC Press, 1932; Reprint: Peter Smith, 1966).

14. William J. Cooper, *Conservative Regime: South Carolina, 1877–1890* (Johns Hopkins Press, 1968).

15. George B. Tindall, *South Carolina Negroes, 1877–1900* (U of SC Press, 1952; Paperback: LSU Press, 1966).

16. Francis B. Simkins, *Pitchfork Ben Tillman: South Carolinian* (LSU Press, 1944; Reprint: Peter Smith, 1964; Paperback: LSU Press, 1967).

17. Ernest M. Lander, *History of South Carolina, 1865–1960* (U of NC Press, 1960; U of SC Press, 1970). Not a monograph, but includes survey of the period since 1900.

Thus far, the only scholarly work of the over-all period is D. D. Wallace, *History of South Carolina* (4 vols.; Amer. Historical Society, 1934), and his not-too-reduced condensation, *South Carolina: A Short History* (U of NC Press, 1951; Reprint: U of SC Press, 1969). Sponsored by the Tricentennial Commission, another one-volume scholarly study will be published in 1972. Lewis P. Jones concluded a "history for laymen," a general "synoptic" history, for the Sandlapper

Press in 1970. Not scholarly but readable is a general narrative: W. Frank Guess, *South Carolina: Annals of Pride and Protest* (Harper & Row, 1960).

GENERAL STUDIES OF THE HISTORY OF THE SOUTH

If one really wants to engage in a "teach-yourself-history" course, perhaps the best way to begin (as in any research undertaking) is to get the over-all picture and then to see where his special interests fit into the larger story. To study South Carolina, one must first know the stories of the United States and of the South.

A quite readable and dependable history of the South has been published by LSU Press since the mid-twentieth century. Naturally, South Carolina plays a significant role in these excellent volumes which include social and economic history as well as political. The ten volumes in this series, *History of the South,* are as follows:

1. Wesley Frank Craven, *Southern Colonies in the Seventeenth Century, 1607–1689* (LSU Press, 1949).

2. Philip Davidson, *Southern Colonies in the Eighteenth Century, 1689–1763.* The only volume in the series not yet (1970) published.

3. John R. Alden, *The South in the Revolution, 1763–1789* (LSU Press, 1957).

4. Thomas P. Abernathy, *The South in the New Nation, 1789–1819* (LSU Press, 1961).

5. Charles S. Sydnor, *Development of Southern Sectionalism, 1819–1848* (LSU Press, 1948; Reprint, 1968; Paperback, 1966).

6. Avery O. Craven, *Growth of Southern Nationalism, 1848–1861* (LSU Press, 1953).

7. E. M. Coulter, *Confederate States of America, 1861–1865* (LSU Press, 1950).

8. E. M. Coulter, *The South During Reconstruction, 1865–1877* (LSU Press, 1947).

4   Introduction

9. C. Vann Woodward, *Origins of the New South, 1877–1913* (LSU Press, 1951; Paperback, 1966).
10. George B. Tindall, *Emergence of the New South, 1913–1945* (LSU Press, 1967).

INTERPRETATIONS OF THE SOUTH

The books listed below relate even less especially to South Carolina, but they contain essays, critical analyses, or "thought pieces" on the history of the South as seen by some of the more perceptive recent scholars.

1. W. J. Cash, *The Mind of the South* (Knopf, 1941; Paperbacks: Doubleday Anchor, 1954; Random Vintage, 1961).
2. Harry S. Ashmore, *Epitaph for Dixie* (Norton, 1958). Written as a sequel to *The Mind of the South*.
3. T. Harry Williams, *Romance and Realism in Southern Politics* (U of Ga Press, 1961; Paperback: LSU Press, 1966).
4. Frank E. Vandiver (ed.), *The Idea of the South: Pursuit of a Central Theme* (U of Chi Press, 1964).
5. Francis B. Simkins, *The Everlasting South* (LSU Press, 1963).
6. Louis D. Rubin and James J. Kilpatrick (eds.), *The Lasting South: Fourteen Southerners Look at Their Home* (Regnery, 1957).
7. Hodding Carter, *Southern Legacy* (LSU Press, 1950; Paperback, 1966).
8. James McBride Dabbs, *Southern Heritage* (Knopf, 1958).
9. James McBride Dabbs, *Who Speaks for the South?* (Funk & Wagnalls, 1964; Paperback: Minerva).

SIGNIFICANT SERIALS

Several serials deserve a special note since they are significant for the reading and study of South Carolina history. They will be cited frequently hereinafter.

The most valuable quarterly is the *South Carolina His-*

torical Magazine, published since the first of the present century by the South Carolina Historical Society, one of the older and more important historical groups in the country. In its earlier years, when it was known as the *South Carolina Historical and Genealogical Magazine,* this periodical devoted much of its space to primary sources, tombstone inscriptions, lists of various groups, etc.; it was thus invaluable to the researcher. In recent years it has included more articles of a secondary nature, based on careful research. The prestigious society behind this valuable magazine is based in the Fireproof Building, Charleston.

The South Carolina Historical Society has also published five bound volumes of papers, cited herein as the S. C. Historical Society *Collections.* Several of these volumes can still be bought, as can back issues of the *South Carolina Historical Magazine* and an index to it.

Another useful and important publication is published as the *Proceedings* of the South Carolina Historical Association, an organization which since its founding in 1931 has been composed of most of the professional historians in the state. The papers read at its annual meetings are subsequently published in the *Proceedings,* which has become an important repository of articles of lasting importance and great usefulness.

Many students overlook a historical gold mine: the *Charleston Year Book,* published for many years by the City of Charleston. Besides contemporary city reports and statistics, it has included both historical data of a primary nature and also many quite significant articles on Charleston history. Too seldom are these volumes consulted, but a library with a file of the *Charleston Year Book* is fortunate indeed.

In 1970, a new periodical was launched which may prove most useful for popular history: *South Carolina History Illustrated,* a hard-bound quarterly. Of less scholarly pretensions has been a magazine begun in 1968, *The Sand-*

lapper: The Magazine of South Carolina, which also carries articles on state history. Some historical articles also appear in the *South Carolina Magazine.*

Articles dealing with South Carolina, of course, are scattered through many scholarly journals, some of which are cited herein.

I

Pre-English Period
(1521–1670)

Section A: SPECIAL STUDIES

1. Paul Quattlebaum, *Land Called Chicora: The Carolinas Under Spanish Rule* (U of Fla Press, 1956). The stress is on the Ayllón ventures, but the author treats all European contacts prior to 1670. Takes up the long controversy of the whereabouts of the River Gualdape and supports the Winyah Bay area.

2. John A. Caruso, *Southern Frontier* (Bobbs-Merrill, 1963), chaps. 4–7. Little new, but a broad survey of the area south of Virginia and east of the Mississippi, 1513–1845. The emphasis is on personalities.

Section B: GENERAL STUDIES

1. Woodbury Lowery, *Spanish Settlements Within the Present Limits of the United States, 1513–1561* (Putnam, 1901; Reprint: Russell, 1959), pp. 3–78 (physical aspects of the land, and the customs and conditions of the natives); pp. 152–71 (Ayllón); pp. 213–52 (DeSoto).

2. Herbert E. Bolton, *Spanish Borderlands* (Yale U Press, 1921; Reprint: U. S. Pubs.), chaps. 1, 3. Includes Ayllón (pp. 12–19) and DeSoto (pp. 46–78).

Section C: GENERAL HISTORIES OF SOUTH CAROLINA

1. David Duncan Wallace, *History of South Carolina* (4 vols.; American Historical Society, 1934), I, chaps. 1–5. This is still the standard history by a remarkable man with

a remarkable grasp of the facts of the story. The most recent
student of state historiography, Elmer D. Johnson, refers
to him by noting, "This careful historian, relying almost
entirely upon original sources and monographic studies, for
the first time placed the history of colonial South Carolina
in proper perspective and gave it accurate treatment." Careful and judicious, but without the trappings of modern
scholarship (e.g., footnotes). Occasional examples of brilliant insight in observations which are not always utterly
objective but which are rendered with judgment and cau-
tion. Viewpoints are often strikingly modern for one trained
in the late 19th century and have often been validated by
events that have transpired since this publication. Prose
often brilliant and clear, but also sometimes marred by
digressions or great detail. The "standard" and best general
South Carolina history. The fourth volume was not pre-
pared by Wallace, but is a wondrously strange collection
of eulogistic biographical sketches; the fee for their inclu-
sion defrayed part of the cost of publication of the history.
(Wallace himself once predicted that in decades hence the
fourth volume would be most valued by scholars for its
information about nonentities about whom nothing else
would be in print.)

2. D. D. Wallace: *South Carolina: A Short History* (U of
NC Press, 1951; Reprint: U of SC Press, 1969), chaps. 1–3.
Condensation of above, but not too much lost thereby.

3. Edward McCrady, *History of South Carolina Under
Proprietary Government, 1670–1719* (Macmillan, 1897; Reprint: Russell, 1969), pp. 39–50. Lengthy history by Bourbon lawyer of Charleston. Amazing storehouse of information here, especially amazing in view of paucity of materials
then easily available to the researcher. Was used extensively
by Wallace. Quite detailed in political history, but sections
on social and institutional history would be especially interesting to modern reader once he had a general idea of the
political history. Quite detailed table of contents, with a
list of topics of each chapter, helps the layman reader to

steer himself into those portions which he thinks would interest him. McCrady was a South Carolina patriot first and a historian second, who writes clearly as a Charlestonian, Episcopalian, ex-Confederate, and lawyer—as Elmer Johnson says in his excellent historiographical study, "A History of South Carolina History to 1789" (unpublished Ph.D. dissertation, University of North Carolina, 1951). McCrady used good sources, although sometimes he stuck too closely to his favorites.

4. Henry Savage, *River of the Carolinas: The Santee* (Rinehart, 1956; Reprint: U of NC Press, 1968), chap. 4. Much broader subject than that indicated by the title. Readable, with many intriguing tales and sidelights. Covers early to modern periods.

5. Yates Snowden, *History of South Carolina* (5 vols.; Lewis Publishing Co., 1920), I, chap. 1. Snowden's history actually consists of two volumes, with the remaining three being a collection of biographical selections which helped to sell the history (like Wallace's fourth volume). Although a delightful person deeply in love with South Carolina (and especially with the Confederacy), Snowden was not basically a professional scholar. Actually he only edited this work in which separate sections were written by various persons (also generally not trained historians) who covered the periods of their special interest. The result is disappointing to those who want an accurate, balanced account by careful, scholarly methods. Instead, this is "simply a glorification of South Carolina in all the stages of its history."

6. Arthur H. Hirsch, *Huguenots of Colonial South Carolina* (Duke U Press, 1928; Reprint: Archon, 1962), chap. 1.

Section D: SPECIAL TOPICS

1. Chapman J. Milling, *Red Carolinians* (U of NC Press, 1940). Actually the book goes through the 18th century with its treatment of Indian groups who lived in South Carolina. The early chapters tell about their life, the later ones about their relations with the white men. Readable, and important.

2. J. G. Johnson, "A Spanish Settlement in South Carolina, 1526," in *Ga. Hist. Qtrly.*, VII (December, 1923),
339–45. Useful article on the Ayllón colony in the Winyah
Bay area, the first European settlement in the state.

3. Mary Ross, "Spanish Settlement of Santa Elena (Port
Royal) in 1578," in *Ga. Hist. Qtrly.*, IX (December, 1925),
352–79. Based on archives material in Seville. Includes map
of Fort San Marcos and a report of a Spanish official who
visited Parris Island in 1578 on an inspection tour. Not
very lively, but there is not too much available on this story.

4. Mary Ross, "With Pardo and Boyano on the Fringes of
the Georgia Land," in *Ga. Hist. Qtrly.*, XIV (December,
1930), 267–85. Rather dull, but included here because there
is so little written on Pardo, who ventured up into the
Piedmont. Includes map of his travels.

5. A. S. Salley, Jr., "Spanish Settlements at Port Royal,
1565–1586," in *S. C. Hist. Mag.*, XXVI (January, 1925),
31–40. Concerned primarily with the controversial question
of just where on Parris Island these settlements were located.
Intriguing for the detective type of historian, but too much
nit-picking for the strictly hammock readers.

6. Virginia C. Holmgren, *Hilton Head* (Hilton Head
Island Publishing Co., 1959), chaps. 1–3. A general history
of an area full of history. Not a work of advanced scholarship, but would be especially interesting to visitors in the
area. Full of names.

7. Sherwood Harris, "Tragic Dream of Jean Ribaut," in
American Heritage, October, 1963, pp. 8 ff. Popular and
readable account of the French in the Port Royal area in
the 1560's.

8. St. Julien Ravenel Childs, "French Origin of Carolina,"
in *Huguenot Society Transactions*, No. 50, pp. 24–44. Treats
both the French of the 1560's and those who began arriving
in the 1680's and 1690's.

Section E: CONTEMPORARY DESCRIPTIONS

(*Note*. There is a great amount of this kind of primary

material on South Carolina. Of great interest also is the great plethora of writings by numerous travelers. Most of this type material is being omitted here, however, since so much of it is rare (although a great many such books are to be found in certain libraries in the state). The reader should remember that this book, basically a layman's guide, in general includes primarily those items obtainable today or those to be found in average libraries.)

1. Katharine M. Jones (ed.), *Port Royal Under Six Flags* (Bobbs-Merrill, 1960), Parts 1-3. A book that provides selected writings of explorers, settlers, visitors, residents, and invaders throughout South Carolina history, but limited to the area around Port Royal and Beaufort. For example, Part 2 (noted here) includes three accounts of the French settlement on Parris Island in 1562: two by René de Laudonniere, and one by Jean Ribaut.

Section F: OLD ACCOUNTS BY EARLY HISTORIANS

1. Alexander Hewat, *An Historical Account of the Rise and Progress of the Colonies of South Carolina and Georgia* (2 vols.; London, 1779; Reprints: (1) As Vol. I of B. R. Carroll, *Historical Collections of South Carolina* (New York, 1836); (2) Spartanburg: The Reprint Co., 1962, in a two-volume edition). Hewat was a Scot who came to Charleston as Presbyterian pastor in 1763. Not sympathetic with the Patriot cause, he returned to England in 1775 but remained interested in South Carolina until his death in 1828. This is the first attempt at a definitive history, but covers only through 1766, with the concentration being on 1700-40. Wordy, Hewat tends to ramble and digress, but his digressions are often valuable; for example, on his treatment of slavery, see Carroll, I, 347-58. Bias: opposed to Proprietors and Anglicans, favorable to royal cause and dissenters. Was much copied by David Ramsay in his *History*. On Hewat himself, see Elmer D. Johnson, "Alexander Hewat: South Carolina's First Historian," in *Jour. Sou. Hist.*, XX (February, 1954), 50-62.

2. William J. Rivers, *A Sketch of the History of South Carolina . . . to 1719* (Charleston, 1856), chaps. 1, 2. (Chap. 2 on the Indians goes much beyond the chronological period included here.) The first really scholarly work on South Carolina. Rivers taught in Charleston and also at South Carolina College. Used good sources and was critical of some of his not-too-careful predecessors. Mostly political history, but has much incidental social and economic history. Generally, it still reads rather well.

3. John Logan, *History of the Upper Country of South Carolina to the Close of the War of Independence* (Charleston, 1859; Reprint: Spartanburg: The Reprint Co., 1960), I, chaps. 1–6. Since Logan did not follow the usual tight chronological method entirely, these chapters move beyond the period of 1521–1670. One can find many astonishing tales and stray bits of information scattered throughout this old book, which is now fortunately available again. In these chapters, for example, one can find descriptions of the country, the natives, the animals, and the natural history— plus later developments after the arrival of Europeans, with personal treatment of many individuals.

Logan was a doctor and educator of Abbeville who felt that the Up-Country had been neglected by historians. Although he used many of the sources available, he did not distinguish clearly between tradition and fact. Almost the first half of the book is natural history, with much on the Indians. After this, he turned to early traders, hunters, and settlers.

The book does not have a very definite arrangement and hence is hard to list within the different sections of this guide. He proposed to write two volumes, but only one was ever published. Hence, the 1960 reprint is still marked Vol. I. (Part of Vol. II was published in the *Historical Collections* of the Jos. Habersham Chapter, D. A. R., Vol. III, 1910.)

II

Enter England
(c. 1663–1685)

Section A: SPECIAL STUDIES

1. M. Eugene Sirmans, *Colonial South Carolina: A Political History, 1663–1763* (U of NC Press, 1966), chaps. 1, 2. The most significant scholarly work on this period, and certainly one of the most important books published in recent years about South Carolina. As the title indicates, it does not include much social, intellectual, or institutional history. Result of much new research into various primary materials. Author was a young scholar at Emory, who died prior to publication.

2. Edward McCrady, *History of South Carolina Under the Proprietary Government, 1670–1719*, chaps. 1–7. Very full, heavy on political history, but not strictly limited to that.

3. Paul Quattlebaum, *Land Called Chicora*, chap. 10.

Section B: GENERAL STUDIES IN SOUTHERN AND AMERICAN HISTORY

1. Wesley Frank Craven, *Southern Colonies in the Seventeenth Century* (LSU Press, 1949), chap. 9. First volume in the most important *History of the South* (10 vols.). Stress is on Chesapeake colonies, but this chapter gives a good condensed story of the beginning of Carolina.

2. Louis B. Wright, *Colonial Search for a Southern Eden* (U of Ala Press, 1953). Charming and entertaining little book (62 pp.) about Elizabethan dreams of an American Utopia, including entertaining quotations from some of the

propaganda designed to lure colonists. Author is a South
Carolinian, as distinguished an authority on this period as
any.

3. Charles M. Andrews, *Colonial Period of American History* (4 vols.; Yale U Press, 1934–38; Paperback), III, chap.
5. Only one of a number of major studies of the colonies,
but one that gives a good coverage to South Carolina.

4. Henry Savage, *River of the Carolinas: The Santee*,
chaps. 5, 6.

Section C: GENERAL HISTORIES OF SOUTH CAROLINA

1. D. D. Wallace, *History of South Carolina*, I, chaps. 6–9.

2. D. D. Wallace, *South Carolina: A Short History*, chaps.
4–6.

3. Yates Snowden, *History of South Carolina*, I, chaps.
2–5.

Section D: SPECIAL TOPICS

1. George C. Rogers, Jr., "First Earl of Shaftesbury"
[Anthony Ashley Cooper, 1621–1683], in *S. C. Hist. Mag.*,
LXVIII (April, 1967), 74–78. The leading Proprietor. A
number of biographies of him also exist.

2. Virginia C. Holmgren, *Hilton Head*, chap. 3.

3. Harriott Horry Ravenel (Mrs. St. Julien Ravenel
Childs, hereinafter listed as Harriott H. Ravenel), *Charleston: The Place and the People* (Macmillan, 1906; Reprints:
Macmillan, 1912 and 1931), chaps. 2, 3. Over-romanticized
with much devotion to legend, but does not claim to be a
full history. Often readable and interesting.

4. Robert G. Rhett, *Charleston: An Epic of Carolina*
(Richmond: Garrett & Massie, 1940), chaps. 2, 3. Covers
much, but is hardly comprehensive. Style simple; little new
for one acquainted with South Carolina history.

5. William A. Courtenay, "Sketch of the History of
Charleston, S. C.," in *Charleston Year Book*, 1880, pp. 241–
320. Includes many statistics and reproductions of early
maps.

6. H. A. M. Smith, "Old Charles Town and Its Vicinity," in *S. C. Hist. Mag.*, XVI (January, 1915), 1–15, and XVI (April, 1915), 49–67. Generally not for the casual reader. Smith also published two other detailed articles on the original Charles Town, including plats and information leading to many of the early property owners: "Charleston: The Original Plan and the Earliest Settlers," in *S. C. Hist. Mag.*, IX (January, 1908), 12–27; and "Charleston and Charleston Neck," in *S. C. Hist. Mag.*, XIX (January, 1918), 3–76.

Section E: CONTEMPORARY DESCRIPTIONS

(*Note:* There is considerable overlapping between these "contemporary descriptions" and some of the old accounts by early historians in the next section.)

1. Three general compilations available:

a. Alex S. Salley (ed.), *Original Narratives of Early Carolina, 1640–1708* (New York, 1911; Reprint: Barnes & Noble, 1967), pp. 1–188. Includes such things as narratives of pre-1670 exploratory voyages, some letters from first colonists, Henry Woodward's account of his trip to visit the Westoes, and three descriptions of Carolina in 1682.

b. Katharine M. Jones (ed.), *Port Royal Under Six Flags*. Part 4 includes accounts of William Hilton (1663), Robert Sandford (1666), and Nichols Carteret (1670).

c. R. B. Carroll, *Historical Collections of South Carolina* (2 vols.; New York, 1836). Still available in many libraries. First volume reprinted Hewat's history (see above). Second volume includes many pamphlets and early descriptions— many readable, many not. Can be viewed both as primary and secondary sources.

2. William Hilton, *A Relation of a Discovery* . . . (London, 1664). Hilton made a voyage along the Carolina coast in 1663 to judge the suitability of the land for settlement and to look into the "nature and temperature of the soyl, the manners and dispositions of the natives, and whatsoever else is remarkable therein." This volume is his account of that.

Reprinted in Salley, *Original Narratives,* pp. 33–61; also, part in Jones, *Port Royal Under Six Flags,* pp. 69–74.

3. Robert Sandford, *A Relation of a Voyage on the Coast of Carolina.* Sandford was "secretary and register" of a Barbadian settlement made on the Cape Fear in 1664. His account was not printed until the 19th century. It is available in the following: *Charleston Year Book,* 1885, pp. 259–96; S. C. Hist. Soc. *Collections,* V, 57–82; Salley, *Original Narratives,* pp. 77–108; Jones, *Port Royal,* pp. 74–79.

4. Robert Horne, *Brief Description of the Province of Carolina* (London, 1666). Gives a good idea of the inducements made to get settlers to come here. Reprinted in Salley, *Original Narratives,* pp. 63–73; also, in Carroll, *Historical Collections,* II, 9–18.

5. Thomas Ashe, *Carolina, or a Description of the Present State of That Country* (London, 1682). Promotional pamphlet; history, description, and propaganda for potential settlers. Reprinted in Carroll, *Historical Collections,* II, 59–84; also, in Salley, *Original Narratives,* pp. 135–60.

6. Samuel Wilson, *Account of the Province of Carolina* (London, 1682). By the secretary to the Proprietors; most widely distributed of the promotional pamphlets which "most strictly kept to the truth." Reprinted in Salley, *Original Narratives,* pp. 161–76; in Carroll, *Historical Collections,* II, 19–35.

7. Maurice Mathews, "A Contemporary View of Carolina in 1680," in *S. C. Hist. Mag.,* LV (July, 1954), 153–59.

8. W. L. Chaffin (ed.), *Extracts from the Diary of Elder William Pratt, Relating to the Founding of a Congregationalist Church at Dorchester in 1695.* Reprinted in Salley, *Original Narratives,* pp. 189–200; also, in *Charleston Year Book,* 1897, pp. 503–12.

9. Langdon Cheves (ed.), "The Shaftesbury Papers and Other Records Relating to Carolina . . . to the Year 1676," in S. C. Hist. Soc. *Collections,* V (1897), 1–476. A treasury of very early documents, letters, reports, and descriptions of the 1660's and 1670's, including Robert Sandford's "The

scription of a Voyage" to Port Royal (1666), statistics and descriptions of the 1669–70 voyage to the founding of English Carolina, and of the first settlement. Includes letters written from Carolina.

Section F: OLD ACCOUNTS BY EARLY HISTORIANS

1. Alexander Hewat, *Historical Account of . . . South Carolina and Georgia.* In the 1960 reprint: I, 25–89; in Carroll, *Historical Collections,* I, 25–89.

2. David Ramsay, *History of South Carolina* (2 vols.; Charleston, 1809; Reprint: Spartanburg: The Reprint Co., 1959), I, 14–19. Ramsay was a Charleston doctor and legislator, one of the first historians of the state, who also did a history of the Revolution. The first of the two volumes was the more historical part of it (much of it on the Revolution), but the second volume is perhaps more valuable to modern readers because of its social and economic history, statistical accounts, and biographical sketches. He relied heavily on Hewat and has been much criticized therefor. (See Elmer D. Johnson, "David Ramsay: Historian or Plagiarist?" in *S. C. Hist. Mag.,* LVII (October, 1956), 189–98.)

3. William J. Rivers, *Sketch of the History of South Carolina,* chaps. 3–5.

4. John Oldmixon, *History of the British Empire in America* (London, 1708). This is a history of the colony to 1706, biased in favor of the Dissenters. Many errors. First chapter deals with discovery and settlement, the second with geographical description. Chapters on Carolina are reprinted in Salley, *Original Narratives,* pp. 313–74; and in Carroll, *Historical Collections,* II, 391–461.

III

The English Colony Matures
(c. 1682–1711)

Section A: SPECIAL STUDIES

1. M. Eugene Sirmans, *Colonial South Carolina*, chaps. 2–5.

2. Verner Crane, *Southern Frontier, 1670–1732* (U of Pa Press, 1929; Paperback: U of Mich Press, 1956). Really a diplomatic and economic history, dealing with English-Indian relations and with the all-important Indian trade and traders. Treats South Carolina not as a separate story but as an outpost of the British Empire, viewing it from London's vantage point.

Section B: GENERAL STUDIES IN SOUTHERN AND AMERICAN HISTORY

1. Charles M. Andrews, *Colonial Period of American History*, III, chap. 4; also chap. 5, pp. 228–39. Scholarly but palatable.

2. Wesley Frank Craven, *Southern Colonies in the Seventeenth Century*, chap. 9.

3. John A. Caruso, *Southern Frontier*, chap. 8.

Section C: GENERAL HISTORIES OF SOUTH CAROLINA

1. D. D. Wallace, *History of South Carolina*, I, chaps. 10–19.

2. D. D. Wallace, *South Carolina: A Short History*, chaps. 6–10.

3. Edward McCrady, *History of South Carolina under the Proprietary Government*, chaps. 10–30.

4. Yates Snowden, *History of South Carolina*, I, chaps. 6–9.

5. William Roy Smith, *South Carolina as a Royal Province* (New York, 1903), chap. 1.

Section D: SPECIAL TOPICS

1. Josephine Pinckney, *Hilton Head* (Farrar & Rinehart, 1941). A historical novel that centers about the colorful Dr. Henry Woodward.

2. Warren B. Smith, *White Servitude in Colonial South Carolina* (U of SC Press, 1961). Deals with indentured servants, a topic often overlooked. On this system in general, see Abbot E. Smith, *Colonists in Bondage: White Servitude and Convict Labor in America, 1607–1776* (U of NC Press, 1947; Reprint: Peter Smith, 1965).

3. Shirley Hughson, *Carolina Pirates and Colonial Commerce, 1670–1740* (Baltimore, 1894). Not as lively as this topic should be, but still "good reading."

4. Louis B. Wright, *Cultural Life in the American Colonies, 1607–1763* (Harper & Row, 1957; Paperback). As title indicates, not limited to any one section or period, but good on South Carolina.

5. William S. Willis, "Divide and Rule: Red, White, and Black in the Southeast," in *Jour. Negro Hist.*, XLVIII (July, 1963), 157–76. On race relations and slavery, and on the connections between slaves and Indians, and the whites' fears of a hostile coalition.

6. Herbert E. Bolton, "Spanish Resistance to the Carolina Traders in Western Georgia, 1680–1704," in *Ga. Hist. Qtrly.*, IX (June, 1925), 115–30.

7. Theodore D. Jervey, "The White Indented Servants of South Carolina," in *S. C. Hist. Mag.*, XII (October, 1911), 163–71.

8. Frank J. Klingberg, *Appraisal of the Negro in Colonial South Carolina* (Washington: Associated Publishers, 1941;

Paperback). An "attempt to consider the Negro as a human
being rather than as an economic factor." Shows conscien-
tious role of early missionaries.

9. J. P. Thomas, "Barbadians in Early South Carolina," in
S. C. Hist. Mag., XXXI (April, 1930), 75–92. Demonstrates
the great influence which this island and its settlers had on
early colonial customs and the course of history. They were
politically influential here as "The Goose Creek Men."

10. Sanford Wilson, "Indian Slavery in the Carolina
Region," in *Jour. Negro Hist.*, XIX (October, 1934), 431–40.

11. J. Leitch Wright, "Spanish Reaction to Carolina," in
N. C. Hist. Rev., XLI (October, 1964), 464–76.

12. A. H. Hirsch, *Huguenots of Colonial South Carolina*
(Duke U Press, 1928; Reprint: Shoe String Press, 1962),
chaps. 3–11.

13. Henry Savage, *River of the Carolinas: The Santee*,
chap. 10. Also on the Huguenots.

14. Harriott H. Ravenel, *Charleston*, chaps. 4–6.

15. Robert G. Rhett, *Charleston*, chaps. 3–5.

Section E: CONTEMPORARY DESCRIPTIONS

1. A. S. Salley (ed.), *Original Narratives of Early Carolina*, pp. 135–313. Nine different descriptions, letters, and
journals written in this era of 1682–1707.

2. John Lawson, *New Voyage to Carolina* (London, 1709;
Reprint: U of NC Press, 1967). A travel account and
natural history by the surveyor-general of North Carolina.
Good on South Carolina plant and animal life, and Indian
civilization. In the new edition, pp. 86–95 tell of his trip
through South Carolina. Also in it, see "The Natural History of Carolina," pp. 96–171. On Lawson, see chap. 7 of
Henry Savage, *River of the Carolinas: The Santee*.

3. Katharine Jones (ed.), *Port Royal Under Six Flags*,
Part 5. On the Cardross settlement (in the Beaufort area in
the 1680's) and its destruction by the Spanish.

4. Herbert E. Bolton, "Spanish Depredations, 1686," in

S. C. Hist. Mag., XXX (April, 1929), 81–89. Bloodcurdling description of the Spanish raid on the Beaufort area.

5. "William Dunlap's Mission to St. Augustine in 1688," in *S. C. Hist. Mag.,* XXXIV (January, 1933), 1–30.

6. G. P. Insch, "Arrival of the Cardross Settlers," in *S. C. Hist. Mag.,* XXX (April, 1929), 69–80. A letter from the first British settlement in the Beaufort area in the 1680's.

Section F: OLD ACCOUNTS BY EARLY HISTORIANS

1. W. J. Rivers, *Sketch of the History of South Carolina,* chaps. 7–10.

2. George Chalmers, *Political Annals of the Present United Colonies* (London, 1779); reprinted in Carroll, *Historical Collections,* II, 274–345. Written by a strong Loyalist, covering only to 1700. Most scholarly account before Rivers. More readable than Hewat.

3. Alexander Hewat: *History of . . . South Carolina and Georgia,* chaps. 3, 4.

4. David Ramsay, *History of South Carolina,* I, 1–52; 70–117.

IV

Internal Dissensions
(c. 1711–1719)

Section A: SPECIAL STUDIES

1. Verner Crane, *Southern Frontier*, chaps. 6–13.
2. M. Eugene Sirmans, *Colonial South Carolina*, chaps. 6–8.
3. Chapman J. Milling, *Red Carolinians*, chaps. 7–9.
4. Robert L. Meriwether, *Expansion of South Carolina, 1729–1765* (Kingsport: Southern Publishers, 1940), chap. 1. Deals with the opening of the backcountry, frontiers, Indian trade. Includes some good descriptive chapters that amount to social history.
5. Shirley Hughson, *Carolina Pirates and Colonial Commerce, 1670–1740*. Most of the action took place about 1718.

Section B: GENERAL STUDIES IN AMERICAN HISTORY

1. Charles M. Andrews, *Colonial Period of American History*, III, 239 ff.

Section C: GENERAL HISTORIES OF SOUTH CAROLINA

1. D. D. Wallace: *History of South Carolina*, I, chaps. 19–29.
2. D. D. Wallace: *South Carolina: A Short History*, chaps. 12–17.
3. W. R. Smith, *South Carolina as a Royal Province*, pp. 11–21.
4. Edward McCrady, *History of South Carolina Under the Proprietary Government*, chaps. 21–31.

5. Edward McCrady, *History of South Carolina Under the Royal Government, 1719–1775* (Macmillan, 1899; Reprint: Russell, 1969), chaps. 1–5.

6. Yates Snowden, *History of South Carolina,* I, chaps. 9–11.

Section D: SPECIAL TOPICS

1. Edward McCrady, *History of South Carolina Under Proprietary Government,* pp. 568–623. On the pirates.

2. Shirley Hughson, *Carolina Pirates and Colonial Commerce, 1670–1740.* Also gives a fair economic history of the times.

3. R. G. Rhett, *Charleston,* chap. 6. This also touches on pirates.

4. Henry Savage, *River of the Carolinas: The Santee.* Chap. 7: on John Lawson; chap. 8: on Carolina traders; chap. 9: on pirates; chap. 11: on rice growing.

5. Chapman J. Milling, *Red Carolinians.* Chaps. 7–9, on the Tuscaroras, the Yamassees, and the Yamassee War; chap. 16: on the Indian trade.

6. Sanford Wilson, "Indian Slavery in the Carolina Region," in *Jour. Negro Hist.,* XIX (October, 1934), 431–40.

7. M. Eugene Sirmans, "Legal Status of the Slave in South Carolina, 1670–1740," in *Jour. Sou. Hist.,* XXVIII (November, 1962), 462–73.

8. Harriott H. Ravenel, *Charleston,* chaps. 5, 6.

9. Richard P. Sherman, *Robert Johnson: Proprietary and Royal Governor of South Carolina* (U of SC Press, 1966).

10. John Caruso, *Southern Frontier,* chap. 8.

11. M. Eugene Sirmans, "Politicians and Planters: The Bull Family of Colonial South Carolina," in S. C. Hist. Assoc. *Procdgs.,* 1962, pp. 32–41.

12. Frank J. Klingberg, "The Mystery of the Lost Yamassee Prince," in *S. C. Hist. Mag.,* LXIII (January, 1962), 18–32. Story of a prince being taken to England for an education and then returned here as part of an interesting but unsuccessful program.

Section E: CONTEMPORARY DESCRIPTIONS

1. Katharine M. Jones (ed.), *Port Royal Under Six Flags,* Part 6. (For the Yemassee War, see pp. 92–102.)

2. *A Narrative of the Proceedings of the People of South Carolina in the Year 1719* (London, 1726); reprinted in B. R. Carroll, *Historical Collections of South Carolina,* II, 141–92. A statement from "Carolina revolutionaries" explaining their secession from Proprietary rule.

Section F: OLD ACCOUNTS BY EARLY HISTORIANS

1. Alexander Hewat, *Historical Account of . . . South Carolina and Georgia* (1962 reprint), I, chaps. 4–6. Also, in Carroll, *Historical Collections,* I.

2. David Ramsay, *History of South Carolina,* I, chaps. 3, 4.

3. W. J. Rivers, *Sketch of the History of South Carolina,* chaps. 9, 10.

V

Expansion of South Carolina
(c. 1730–1765)

Section A: SPECIAL STUDIES

1. Robert L. Meriwether, *Expansion of South Carolina, 1729–1765* (Kingsport: Southern Publishers, 1940). A significant and valuable book but not a lively one. Trade and traders, settlers and settlements, with good view of the backcountry as the townships promoted the influx of newcomers.

2. M. Eugene Sirmans, *Colonial South Carolina,* chaps. 8, 9, 11.

3. Carl Bridenbaugh, *Myths and Realities: Societies of the Colonial South* (LSU Press, 1952; Reprint: Peter Smith, 1968; Paperback: Atheneum, 1963). Superb and readable little book. On this era, see chap. 2, "The Back Settlements."

3. Edward McCrady, *History of South Carolina Under the Royal Government,* chaps. 6–14; 16, 17.

Section B: GENERAL HISTORIES OF SOUTH CAROLINA

1. D. D. Wallace, *History of South Carolina,* I, chaps. 31–35; II, chap. 43.

2. D. D. Wallace, *South Carolina: A Short History,* chaps. 18–20; 24.

3. Yates Snowden, *History of South Carolina,* I, chaps. 12–15.

Section C: SPECIAL TOPICS

1. Richard P. Sherman: *Robert Johnson: Proprietary and*

Royal Governor of South Carolina. Deals with one of the most amazing governors who put the province on the road to prosperity and political stability after 1729.

2. Verner W. Crane, "A Lost Utopia of the First American Frontier," in *Sewanee Review,* XXVII (January, 1919), 48–61. On the remarkable career of Christian Gottlieb Priber.

3. Knox Millan, "Christian Priber and the Jesuit Myth," in *S. C. Hist. Mag.,* LXI (April, 1960), 75–81.

4. Verner W. Crane, *Southern Frontier.*

5. Josiah Moffatt, "The Scotch-Irish of the Up-Country," in *So. Atl. Qtrly.,* XXXIII (April, 1934), 137–51.

6. James G. Leyburn, *The Scotch-Irish: A Social History* (U of NC Press, 1962). An excellent and useful book; not limited to South Carolina.

7. W. H. Wannamaker, "German Element in the Settlement of the South," in *So. Atl. Qtrly.,* IX (April, 1910), 144–55. Naturally, many of the topics noted herein can also be found in various local histories, which necessarily are being omitted from this guide. On the topic of Wannamaker's article, for example, there certainly would be more about Germans in histories of Newberry and Orangeburg.

8. Phinzy Spalding, "South Carolina and Georgia: The Early Days," in *S. C. Hist. Mag.,* LXIX (April, 1968), 83–96. On early relations, in the 1730's.

9. Robert G. Rhett, *Charleston,* chaps. 7, 9.

10. Harriott H. Ravenel, *Charleston,* chaps. 8, 9.

11. H. A. M. Smith, "Beaufort: The Original Plan and the First Settlers," in *S. C. Hist. Mag.,* IX (July, 1908), 141–60.

12. H. A. M. Smith, "Georgetown: The Original Plan and the First Settlers," in *S. C. Hist. Mag.,* IX (April, 1908), 85–101.

13. H. A. M. Smith, "Purrysburgh," in *S. C. Hist. Mag.,* X (October, 1909), 187–219. One of the first of the townships, settled by the German Swiss, now a ghost town.

14. Douglas Brown, *The Catawba Indians* (U of SC Press, 1966). Not limited to this period, but a general history of this group. Disappointing; not as attractive or as valuable as Milling, *Red Carolinians*, mentioned earlier.

15. Gilbert P. Voight, "Religious Conditions among German-Speaking Settlers in South Carolina, 1732-1744," in *S. C. Hist. Mag.*, LVI (April, 1955), 59–66.

Section D: CONTEMPORARY DESCRIPTIONS

1. Charles Woodmason, *Carolina Backcountry on the Eve of the Revolution* (U of NC Press, 1953; Paperback, 1969). Most significant and frequently cited book. Woodmason was an Anglican missionary, whose pungent remarks in his journal and his candid observations constitute an enjoyable and helpful record of the not very civilized backcountry.

2. James Glen, *A Description of South Carolina* (London, 1761); Reprint in C. J. Milling (ed.), *Colonial South Carolina: Two Contemporary Descriptions* (U of SC Press, 1951), pp. 3–104; also included in Carroll, *Historical Collections,* II, 193–272. Valuable view of the state by one of its best governors, who traveled widely over the area. Careful survey, based on facts and firsthand information. Discussed geography, agriculture, government; gave statistics on trade and shipping.

3. Dr. George Milligan, *A Short Description of the Province of South Carolina* (London, 1770); Reprint in Milling (ed.), *Colonial South Carolina*, pp. 111–206. Written in 1763. Valuable on diseases. Has much meteorological data.

4. James Adair, *History of the American Indian* (London, 1775). Reprints: in Samuel C. Williams (ed.), *History of the American Indian* (Johnson City: Watauga Press, 1930); Johnson, 1969. On the Cherokees, see pp. 237–73 of the 1930 edition.

5. R. W. Kelsey (ed.), "Swiss Settlers in South Carolina," in *S. C. Hist. Mag.*, XXIII (July, 1922), 85–91. Contemporary letters describing Purrysburgh.

6. Joseph W. Barnwell (ed.), "Fort King George: Journal

of Col. John Barnwell in the Construction of the Fort on the Altmaha in 1721," in *S. C. Hist. Mag.*, XXVII (October, 1926), 189–203. Description of quite an epic—construction of a fort in an inhospitable area, part of "Tuscarora Jack's" plan to build a peripheral defense system or, if he looked at the Spanish, as part of a "containment policy."

7. David Humphreys, *History of the Propagation of the Gospel in Foreign Parts* (London, 1729). Section on South Carolina included in Carroll, *Historical Collections,* II, 537–68. Much information on slaves, Indians, and the economy in a description of the missionary work of the Society for the Propagation of the Gospel early in the 18th century.

8. *Proposals by Mr. Peter Purry . . . and a Description of the Province of South Carolina Drawn up at Charles-Town in September, 1731* (1731), reprinted in Carroll, *Historical Collections,* II, 121–40. Utopia, as described fascinatingly by a promoter.

9. "Report of the Committee . . . on the St. Augustine Expedition under General Oglethorpe" (1740), in S. C. Hist. Soc. *Collections,* IV (1887), 1–178.

10. *The St. Augustine Expedition of 1740: A Report of the South Carolina General Assembly* (Charleston, 1741). Reprint (from *The Colonial Records of South Carolina*), edited by John Tate Lanning (U of SC Press, 1954).

Section E: OLD ACCOUNTS BY EARLY HISTORIANS

1. John H. Logan, *History of the Upper Country of South Carolina,* I, chaps. 8–14.

2. David Ramsay, *History of South Carolina,* I, chaps. 8–14.

3. Alexander Hewat, *Historical Account . . . of South Carolina and Georgia,* II, chaps. 7–9.

4. Alexander Gregg, *History of the Old Cheraws* (New York, 1867; Reprints: Columbia: The State Co., 1905; Spartanburg: The Reprint Co., 1905), chaps. 2–5. Gregg, al-

though trained as a lawyer, became a minister and served as rector in Cheraw. He reprinted much original material. Much of the work is genealogical, but it contains useful information on the Indians in the northern part of the state and a particularly good account of the Regulator movement of the 1760's. Gregg wrote the book after he had moved to Texas where he was an Episcopal bishop.

VI

The Cherokee War (c. 1740–1765)

Section A: SPECIAL STUDIES

1. David H. Corkran, *Cherokee Frontier: Conflict and Survival, 1740–1762* (U of Okla Press, 1962). First-rate monograph with refreshing approach—from the Indian viewpoint.

2. John Alden, *John Stuart and the Southern Colonial Frontier* (U of Mich Press, 1944; Reprint: Gordian, 1966). A detailed and impressive piece of scholarship. Stuart was the British Southern Indian superintendent for a number of years, responsible for British-Indian relations over much of the southeastern area of the continent. Subtitle of the book tells much about it: *A Study of Indian Relations, War, Trade, and Land Problems in the Southern Wilderness, 1754–1775.*

3. M. Eugene Sirmans, *Colonial South Carolina*, chaps. 12–15.

4. Robert L. Meriwether, *Expansion of South Carolina*, chaps. 13–16.

Section B: GENERAL HISTORIES OF SOUTH CAROLINA

1. D. D. Wallace, *History of South Carolina*, II, chaps. 41–42.

2. D. D. Wallace, *South Carolina: A Short History*, chaps. 20, 21.

3. Edward McCrady, *History of South Carolina Under Royal Government*, chaps. 14, 16–19.

4. Yates Snowden, *History of South Carolina*, I, chaps. 16, 17.

Section C: SPECIAL TOPICS

1. Philip M. Hamer, "Anglo-French Rivalry in the Cherokee Country, 1754-1757," in *N. C. Hist. Rev.*, II (July, 1925), 303–22.

2. Philip M. Hamer, "Fort Loudoun in the Cherokee War, 1758-1761," in *N. C. Hist. Rev.*, II (October, 1925), 442–58.

3. Chapman J. Milling, *Red Carolinians*, chaps. 14, 15.

4. Grace Steele Woodward, *The Cherokees* (U of Okla Press, 1963; Reprint, 1965), chaps. 1–4. This section covers their story down to the Revolution.

5. Chapman J. Milling, *Exile Without End* (Columbia: Bostick & Thornley, 1943). Gripping story of the Acadians (French) transported to Charleston in 1755, who stayed in the colony about five years.

Section D: CONTEMPORARY DESCRIPTIONS

1. Henry Timberlake, *Memoirs, 1756–65* (Marietta, Ga.: Continental Book Co., 1948). Timberlake was a British officer who participated in the Indian difficulties at the time of the French and Indian War.

2. Samuel C. Williams (ed.), *Early Travels in the Tennessee Country, 1540–1800* (Johnson City: Watauga Press, 1928). Contains many interesting accounts by travelers, including some who participated in the Indian wars that involved South Carolina.

Section E: OLD ACCOUNTS BY EARLY HISTORIANS

1. Alexander Hewat, *Historical Account of . . . South Carolina and Georgia*, chap. 10; also, reprinted in Carroll, *Historical Collections*, I, 426–78.

2. J. B. O. Landrum, *Colonial and Revolutionary History of Upper South Carolina* (Greenville, 1897; Reprint: Spartanburg: The Reprint Co., 1962), chaps. 1–6. Landrum was a Baptist preacher in the Spartanburg area; when he wrote this, he had moved to Oklahoma where he was a missionary and a teacher. It was more compilation than original work, "renewing chronicles of the past," as he put it.

3. John H. Logan, *History of the Upper Country of South Carolina*, I, chaps. 15–20.

VII

Age of Aristocracy
(18th Century)

Section A: SPECIAL STUDIES

1. Carl Bridenbaugh, "Carolina Society," chap. 2 in *Myths and Realities*. Excellent and readable social history.

2. George C. Rogers, Jr., *Charleston in the Age of the Pinckneys* (U of Okla Press, 1969). Admirable brief study, concerned mainly with the late 18th and the early 19th centuries. Provides insight based on sound scholarship rather than legends.

3. F. P. Bowes, *Culture of Early Charleston* (U of NC Press, 1942). At the time of its publication, this monograph was perhaps the best book on the subject. Careful, concise, well-written examination of social history; book is still available.

4. Robert G. Rhett, *Charleston*, chap. 8.

5. Harriott H. Ravenel, *Charleston*, chaps. 7–9.

6. M. Eugene Sirmans, "The Colony at Mid-Century," chap. 10 in *Colonial South Carolina*. Good general overview of the colony inserted into this otherwise strictly political history.

Section B: GENERAL STUDY IN SOUTHERN HISTORY

1. John Alden, "Peoples and Their Pursuits" and "The Social Scene," chaps. 2 and 3 in *The South in the Revolution, 1763–1789* (LSU Press, 1957).

Section C: GENERAL HISTORIES OF SOUTH CAROLINA

1. D. D. Wallace, *History of South Carolina,* I, chaps.
36–39.
2. D. D. Wallace, *South Carolina: A Short History,* chaps.
22, 23.
3. Edward McCrady, *History of South Carolina Under the
Royal Government,* chaps. 20–26.

Section D: SPECIAL TOPICS: (1) SLAVERY IN THE COLONIAL
ERA

1. Elizabeth Donnan, "Slave Trade into South Carolina
Before the Revolution," in *Amer. Hist. Rev.,* XXXIII (July,
1928), 804–28. The definitive scholarship on the "foreign
slave trade" of the colonial period.
2. Marguerite B. Hamer, "A Century Before Manumission
—Sidelights on Slavery in Mid-18th Century South Carolina," *N. C. Hist. Rev.,* XVII (July, 1940), 232–36.
3. Frank J. Klingberg, *An Appraisal of the Negro in
Colonial South Carolina* (Associated Publishers, 1941),
chaps. 2–6.
4. William A. Schaper, "Sectionalism and Representation
in South Carolina," in American Historical Association,
Annual Report, 1900, I, 287–324; Reprint (as separate
book): Da Capo Press, 1968, with same page numbers. An
essay on the labor system of the Low Country.
5. Sanford Winston, "Indian Slavery in the Carolina Region," in *Jour. Negro Hist.,* XIX (October, 1934), 431–40. A
topic even less well-known than that of Negro slavery.
6. Winthrop Jordan, *White Over Black: American Attitudes Toward the Negro, 1550–1812* (U of NC Press, 1968;
Paperback: Penguin, 1969). Pulitzer Prize winner.
7. Edgar L. Pennington, "The Reverend Le Jau's Work
Among the Indians and Negro Slaves," in *Jour. Sou. Hist.,*
I (November, 1935), 442–58. A useful biographical sketch
of an important missionary of the S. P. G. His journal
of 1706–17 is also available: *Carolina Chronicle,* edited by
Frank J. Klingberg (U of Calif Press, 1956, Paperback)

8. General books on slavery are numerous—and getting more so all the time. See, for example, Kenneth M. Stampp, *The Peculiar Institution* (Knopf, 1956; Paperback, Random Vintage, 1964). Older, and reflecting a different viewpoint, is U. B. Phillips, *American Negro Slavery* (Appleton, 1918; Reprint: Peter Smith, 1959; Paperback, LSU Press, 1966).

Section D: SPECIAL TOPICS: (2) COLONIAL ECONOMIC HISTORY

1. Leila Sellers, *Charleston Business on the Eve of the Revolution* (U of NC Press, 1934). A monograph on a topic which can hardly be lively but which is important.

2. Carl Bridenbaugh, *Cities in the Wilderness: Urban Life in America, 1625–1742* (Knopf, 1955; Paperback: Capricorn, 1964). Appropriate, since South Carolina in this era was basically a city-state.

3. Henry DeSaussure Bull, "Ashley Hall Plantation," in *S. C. Hist. Mag.*, LIII (April, 1952), 61–66. One of the now gone major plantations, home of Lt. Gov. William Bull.

4. Richard M. Jellison, "Paper Currency in Colonial South Carolina: A Reappraisal," in *S. C. Hist. Mag.*, LXII (July, 1961), 134–47. A thorny topic that plagues many readers of the general histories of the state; this article can be helpful for such students.

5. Richard Walsh, "Charleston Mechanics: A Brief Study, 1760–1776," in *S. C. Hist. Mag.*, LX (July, 1959), 123–44. The group prominent in the "Sons of Liberty," generally followers of Christopher Gadsden.

6. C. Robert Haywood, "Mercantilism and South Carolina Agriculture, 1700-1763," in *S. C. Hist. Mag.*, LX (January, 1959), 15–27. One will discover here the evidence that New Deal ideas and procedures did not have to wait for the 20th century to make their appearance.

7. L. C. Gray, *History of Agriculture in the Southern United States* (2 vols.; Carnegie Institution, 1933; Reprints: Peter Smith, 1953; Kelley, 1969), I, 94–95; 119–20; 155–57; 280–97. The standard study on this important topic. All South Carolina crops can be studied here.

8. Harriott H. Ravenel, *Eliza Lucas Pinckney* (Scribner's, 1896; Reprint: Spartanburg: The Reprint Co., 1967). Included here because of her pioneer work in agriculture. Also, see fictionalized biography: Nell S. Graydon, *Eliza of Wappoo* (Columbia: R. L. Bryan, 1967).

9. Verner W. Crane, "Charleston Indian Trade," chap. 5 in *Southern Frontier*. Most people think of South Carolina economy in the colonial period only in terms of agriculture; such is in error, for this Indian trade was the first bonanza for the colony.

Section D: SPECIAL TOPICS: (3) INTELLECTUAL AND CULTURAL

1. Anne King Gregorie, "First Decade of the Charleston Library Society," in S. C. Hist. Assoc. *Procdgs.*, 1935, pp. 3–10.

2. Edward McCrady, "Education in South Carolina Prior to and During the Revolution," in S. C. Hist. Soc. *Collections*, IV (1887), 10–54.

3. J. Harold Easterby, *History of the College of Charleston* (Charleston, 1935), chap. 1.

4. George C. Rogers, Jr., *Church and State in 18th Century South Carolina* (Charleston: Dalcho Historical Society, 1959). All of the major denominations also have histories of their work in South Carolina.

5. Andrew T. Nelson, "'Enthusiasm' in Carolina, 1740," in *So. Atl. Qtrly.*, XLIV (October, 1945), 397–407. The story of the collisions between the Reverends George Whitefield and Alexander Garden.

6. William H. Kinney III, "Alexander Garden and George Whitefield: The Significance of Revivalism in South Carolina, 1738–1741," in *S. C. Hist. Mag.*, LXXI (January, 1970), 1–16.

7. Hennig Cohen, *South Carolina Gazette, 1732–1775* (U of SC Press, 1953). A useful study of the leading colonial newspaper, but a book that is much broader than just that, as it gives much insight into colonial life.

8. W. L. King, *Newspaper Press of Charleston* (Charleston, 1872), chaps. 1–3.

9. Gilbert P. Voight, "Cultural Contributions of German Settlers to South Carolina," in *S. C. Hist. Mag.*, LIII (October, 1952), 183–89.

10. E. D. Seeber, "French Theater in Charleston in the 18th Century," in *S. C. Hist. Mag.*, XLII (January, 1941), 1–7.

11. Hugh F. Rankin, *Theater in Colonial America* (U of NC Press, 1965), *passim.*

12. Robert A. Law, "Charleston Theaters, 1736-66," in *Nation*, XCIX (September 3, 1914), 278–79.

13. Robert Wilson, "Art and Artists in Provincial South Carolina," in *Charleston Year Book*, 1899, pp. 137–47.

Section D: SPECIAL TOPICS: (4) GENERAL AND MISCELLANEOUS

1. D. H. Bacot, "South Carolina Middle Country at the End of the Eighteenth Century," in *So. Atl. Qtrly.*, XXIII (January, 1924), 50–66. Good social history, much of it drawn from travelers' accounts and contemporary accounts.

2. D. H. Bacot, "South Carolina Up-Country at the End of the Eighteenth Century," in *Amer. Hist. Rev.*, XXVIII (July, 1923), 682–98. Strictly social history.

3. Robert L. Meriwether, "The Back-Country in 1759," chap. 13 in *Expansion of South Carolina*. A good, condensed description by an authority.

4. John Duffy, "Yellow Fever in Colonial Charleston," in *S. C. Hist. Mag.*, LII (October, 1951), 189–97.

5. John Duffy, "Eighteenth Century Health Conditions," in *Jour. Sou. Hist.*, XVII (August, 1952), 289–302.

6. Joseph I. Waring, *History of Medicine in South Carolina, 1670–1825* (S. C. Medical Association, 1964). Sound social history which naturally touches on various aspects of Carolina life. Contains many biographical sketches and a useful appendix.

7. Julia Spruill, "Virginia and Carolina Homes Before

the Revolution," in *N. C. Hist. Rev.,* XII (October, 1935), 320–40.

8. T. P. Lesesne, *Landmarks of Charleston* (Richmond: Garrett & Massie, 1932). What the name implies. With its information on specific houses and buildings, useful for a walking tour of the historic port city. Such helpful information is also handily available in two more recent guidebooks: Samuel G. Stoney, *This Is Charleston* (Carolina Art Association, 1944), and *Across the Cobblestones* (Junior League of Charleston, 1965).

9. Frank Ryan, "Travelers in South Carolina in the Eighteenth Century," in *Charleston Year Book,* 1945, pp. 208–56. Invaluable synthesis, telling something of the travels and travelers, and the major aspects and attributes of these useful observers. Provocative for the interested student since it gives useful "leads" for locating travel accounts which one might want to pursue further. Some accounts constitute one of the most entertaining ways of reading history and of "getting the feel" of the different periods. Fortunately, many of the accounts mentioned here have been reprinted in the 1960's (and are noted in the present booklet). For descriptions in the Ryan study, see chap. 2, "The City," and chap. 3, "The Country."

Section E: CONTEMPORARY DESCRIPTIONS

1. John Drayton, *A View of South Carolina* (Charleston, 1802; Reprint: University Microfilms, 1966). A much quoted and often cited observation by an early governor. Valuable, but not as easy reading as some of the more modern secondary sources.

2. Joseph W. Barnwell (ed.), "Diary of Timothy Ford, 1785–86," in *S. C. Hist. Mag.,* XIII (July, 1912), 132–47; and XIII (October, 1912), 181–204. A delightful view of the state written by a keen and cultured newcomer who moved here just before the Revolution and who had entree to the charmed circles of the aristocracy.

3. John Bennett (ed.), "Charleston as Described in 1774 by an English Traveler," in *S. C. Hist. Mag.*, XLVII (July, 1946), 179–80.

4. James Sutherland, "Letter from a British Officer Describing Charleston, 1729–1731," in *S. C. Hist. Mag.*, LXVIII (April, 1967), 79–84.

5. Thomas J. Tobias (ed.), "Charles Town in 1764," in *S. C. Hist. Mag.*, LVII (January, 1956), 63–74. Letters written from the town at that time by a New England visitor.

These are but samples. Many more are readily available in print, and large numbers of travelers' accounts are being published or reprinted. In connection with such, consider the already noted article by Frank Ryan, "Travelers in South Carolina in the Eighteenth Century," in *Charleston Year Book*, 1945, p). 208–56.

Section F: OLD ACCOUNTS BY EARLY HISTORIANS

1. David Ramsay, *History of South Carolina*, II, chaps. 5–10. Now probably the more valuable portion of this famed old history. Intriguing observations about the economy, agriculture, virtues, and vices of the people. Quite readable.

2. Alexander Hewat, *Historical Account of the Rise and Progress of the Colonies of South Carolina and Georgia.* For this section, see the 1962 reprint edition, II, 131–91; 288–307; in the reprint contained in Carroll, *Historical Collections*, see I, 379–425; 500–15.

3. Edward McCrady, "Slavery in the Province of South Carolina," in American Historical Association, *Annual Report*, 1895, pp. 629–73.

4. Harvey T. Cook, *Rambles in the Pee Dee Basin of South Carolina* (Columbia: The State Co., 1926).

VIII

Coming of the Revolution
(1763–1775)

Section A: SPECIAL STUDIES

1. Richard Walsh, *Charleston's Sons of Liberty: A Study of the Artisans, 1763–1789* (U of SC Press, 1959; Paperback).

2. William M. Dabney and Marion Dargan, *William Henry Drayton and the American Revolution* (U of N Mex Press, 1962). Since no definitive monograph of this period has yet been published, biographies provide one approach to reading about it. Oxford-educated Drayton was a revolutionary propagandist and an eloquent spokesman for the Revolutionary cause. His impressive career was cut short by his death in 1779 at the age of thirty-seven.

3. D. D. Wallace, *Life of Henry Laurens* (Putnam, 1915; Reprint: Russell, 1967). Still the definitive study on one of the most important and impressive statesmen yet produced by the state. *The Papers of Henry Laurens* are now (1970) in process of being published (U of SC Press).

4. Richard Barry, *Mr. Rutledge of South Carolina* (Duell, Sloan & Pearce, 1942). Quite readable, but the author claims too much for his subject—so much so, that one reviewer questioned whether it should be shelved as history or fiction. Useful, if read with reservation.

5. Marvin R. Zahniser, *Charles Cotesworth Pinckney* (U of NC Press, 1967). Another key figure, presented in an excellent and scholarly biography which seems to show the subject as being a "level-headed moderate man."

6. Richard M. Brown, *South Carolina Regulators* (Harvard U Press, 1963). A study of the significant backcountry discontent which came to a head and almost to violence in the 1760's—and had much to do finally with the Piedmont attitude toward the colonial controversy with the mother country.

Section B: GENERAL STUDIES IN SOUTHERN AND AMERICAN HISTORY

1. John R. Alden, *The South in the Revolution, 1763–1789* (LSU Press, 1957), chaps. 4–10.

2. John C. Miller, *Origins of the American Revolution* (Little, Brown, 1943; Stanford, 1957; Paperback: Stanford U Press). Readable, popular, breezy account, not limited to South Carolina. Includes good anecdotes.

3. L. H. Gipson, *Coming of the Revolution, 1763–1775* (Harper & Row, 1954; Paperback). Distinguished historian's work, written from the imperial viewpoint. Product of a multi-volume work by this scholar.

4. A. M. Schlesinger, *The Colonial Merchants and the American Revolution* (New York, 1918; Reprint: Ungar, 1957; Paperback: Atheneum, 1968). Again not limited to South Carolina, but useful because of the important role played by certain Charleston businessmen, such as Christopher Gadsden.

Section C: GENERAL HISTORIES OF SOUTH CAROLINA

1. D. D. Wallace, *History of South Carolina*, II, chaps. 43–50.

2. D. D. Wallace, *South Carolina: A Short History*, chaps. 24–28.

3. Edward McCrady, *History of South Carolina Under the Royal Government*, chaps. 27–41.

4. W. Roy Smith, *South Carolina as a Royal Province*, pp. 330–405.

5. Yates Snowden, *History of South Carolina*, I, chaps. 18–22.

42   Coming of the Revolution

Section D: SPECIAL TOPICS

1. Robert H. Woody, "Christopher Gadsden and the Stamp
Act," in S. C. Hist. Assoc. *Procdgs.*, 1939, pp. 3–12. Gadsden,
being South Carolina's Sam Adams, was a key figure in this
commotion.

2. Richard Walsh, "Christopher Gadsden: Radical or Conservative Revolutionary?" in *S. C. Hist. Mag.*, LXIII
(October, 1962), 195–203.

3. Richard Walsh (ed.), *The Writings of Christopher
Gadsden, 1746–1805* (U of SC Press, 1966).

4. Harriott H. Ravenel, *Eliza Pinckney*.

5. Gary D. Olson, "Loyalists and the American Revolution: Thomas Brown and the South Carolina Backcountry,
1775-1776," in *S. C. Hist. Mag.*, LXVIII (October, 1967),
201–19; LXIX (January, 1968), 44–56. Brown was an intriguing leader of the numerous backcountry Loyalists who
frustrated the efforts of William Henry Drayton and William
Tennent to swing this group over to the Patriot cause. This
article gives good insight into conditions and feelings in
the Piedmont.

6. Philip Davidson, "Southern Backcountry on the Eve
of the Revolution," pp. 1–14 in Avery O. Craven (ed.),
Essays in Honor of William E. Dodd (U of Chi Press, 1935).

7. Jack P. Greene, "Bridge to the Revolution: The Wilkes
Fund Controversy in South Carolina, 1769–1775," in *Jour.
Sou. Hist.*, XXIX (February, 1963), 19–52. This thorny con-
troversy, not itself strictly an American issue, embroiled
South Carolina's colonial leadership in a feud with England
which made them more prone to ally themselves with other
Americans agitated with the mother country for other
reasons and about other policies.

8. Frank W. Ryan, "The Role of South Carolina in the
First Continental Congress," in *S. C. Hist. Mag.*, LX (July,
1959), 147–63.

9. Marguerite Steedman, "Charleston's Forgotten Tea
Party," in *Ca. Rev*, XXI (Summer, 1967), 244-59.

Section E: CONTEMPORARY DESCRIPTIONS

1. "Journal of Reverend William Tennent," in *Charleston Year Book*, 1894, pp. 295–312. An account of the Drayton-Tennent trip of 1775 designed to convert the backcountry Loyalists to the Patriot cause; the attempt was a failure. The bushwhacking is also described in two early accounts: David Ramsay, *History of the Revolution in South Carolina* (2 vols.; Trenton, 1785; Reprint: Russell, 1968), I, 70 ff.; and Robert W. Gibbes (ed.), *Documentary History of the Revolution in South Carolina* (3 vols.; New York, 1853–57), in Vol. I. Especially in letters to backcountry leaders, some insight of the problem can be gained in "Journal of the Council of Safety for the Province of South Carolina. 1775," in S. C. Hist. Soc. *Collections* (1858), II.

2. James H. O'Donnell (ed.), "A Loyalist View of the Drayton-Tennent-Hart Mission to the Upcountry," in *S. C. Hist. Mag.*, LXVII (January, 1966), 15–28. Thomas Brown's observations on this mission which was designed to win the backwoodsmen over to support the Council of Safety.

3. B. D. Bargar (ed.), "Charles Town Loyalism in 1775: The Secret Reports of Alexander Innes," in *S. C. Hist. Mag.*, LXIII (July, 1962), 125–36.

4. John Bennett (ed.), "Charleston in 1774 as Described by an English Traveler," in *S. C. Hist. Mag.*, XLVII (July, 1946), 179–80.

5. Katharine M. Jones (ed.), *Port Royal Under Six Flags*, Part 7.

Section F: OLD ACCOUNTS BY EARLY HISTORIANS

1. J. B. O. Landrum, *Colonial and Revolutionary History of Upper South Carolina*, chaps. 7–11. Not a great history, but at least useful if one first reads some of the modern accounts. Chap. 11 treats the interesting story of "The Famous Snow Campaign."

2. Alexander Hewat, *Historical Account of . . . South Carolina and Georgia*, chap. 11 (in both the 1962 Hewat

reprint and the 1836 reprint in Carroll, *Historical Collections*, I).

3. Alexander Gregg, *History of the Old Cheraws*, chaps. 6–11.

4. John Drayton, *Memoirs of the American Revolution* (2 vols.; Charleston, 1821; Reprint: Arno, 1960). Mostly drawn from the notes and manuscripts of his father, William Henry Drayton, the "propagandist of revolution." Includes a biographical sketch of William H. Drayton. Detailed account, beginning in 1753 and nearly all devoted to the period before the Revolutionary War.

5. David Ramsay, *History of South Carolina*, I, 124–62. Perhaps Ramsay's most significant work, now reissued.

Note: Readers are reminded that bibliographical data about a title are included the first time the title is listed in this guide but normally are not repeated each time that book is mentioned again.

IX

The American Revolution (1775–1783)

Section A: SPECIAL STUDIES

1. Mildred F. Treacy, *Prelude to Yorktown: Southern Campaigns of Nathanael Greene, 1780–81* (U of NC Press, 1963). Clear, readable, interesting, with much of the action in South Carolina. Very useful.

2. Burke Davis, *The Cowpens-Guilford Courthouse Campaign* (Lippincott, 1962). Intriguing tale told with verve in good journalistic fashion.

Section B: GENERAL STUDIES IN SOUTHERN AND AMERICAN HISTORY

Obviously, most histories of the Revolution will have sections on South Carolina. This list attempts only to offer a sampling.

1. John R. Alden, *The South in the Revolution,* chaps. 11–16. This volume in the distinguished *History of the South* series has one of the best accounts of the South Carolina role.

2. *American Heritage Book of the Revolution* (American Heritage, 1958). Satisfactory, but does not contain much on South Carolina.

3. John C. Miller, *Triumph of Freedom* (Little, Brown, 1948; Paperback). A popular, quite readable as well as scholarly study.

4. Richard B. Morris, *Making of a Nation* (Time-Life, 1963).

5. Howard H. Peckham, *The War for Independence* (U of Chi Press, 1958; Paperback).

6. Claude Van Tyne, *Loyalists in the Revolution* (Macmillan, 1902; Reprint: Peter Smith, 1959).

7. Christopher Ward, *The War of the Revolution,* ed. John R. Alden (2 vols.; Macmillan, 1952), chaps. 57–79.

Section C: GENERAL HISTORIES OF SOUTH CAROLINA

1. D. D. Wallace, *History of South Carolina,* II, chaps. 51–67.

2. D. D. Wallace, *South Carolina: A Short History,* chaps. 29–34.

3. Yates Snowden, *History of South Carolina,* I, Part 3.

4. Edward McCrady, *History of South Carolina in the Revolution,* (2 vols.; Macmillan, 1901–02; Reprint: Russell, 1969).

Section D: SPECIAL TOPICS: (1) GENERAL

1. Chapman J. Milling, *Red Carolinians,* chap. 16. The Indian phase of the war—a threat from the Cherokees early in the war.

2. George W. Kyte, "General Greene's Plans for the Capture of Charleston, 1781–82," in *S. C. Hist. Mag.,* LXII (April, 1961), 96–106.

3. George W. Kyte, "Victory in the South: an Appraisal of General Greene's Strategy in the Carolinas," in *N. C. Hist. Rev.,* XXXVII (July, 1960), 321–48.

4. Robert C. Pugh, "Revolutionary Militia in the Southern Campaign, 1780–81," in *Wm. & Mary Qtrly.,* XIV (April, 1957), 154–75.

5. Robert G. Rhett, *Charleston,* chaps. 12–14.

6. Harriott H. Ravenel, *Charleston,* chaps. 13–17.

7. E. P. Levett, "Loyalism in Charleston, 1761–1784," in *S. C. Hist. Assoc. Procdgs.,* 1936, pp. 3–17.

8. Robert W. Barnwell, "Migration of Loyalists from South Carolina," in *S. C. Hist. Assoc. Procdgs.,* 1937, pp. 34–41.

9. A. C. M. Azay, "Palmetto Fort, Palmetto Flag," in *American Heritage*, October, 1955.

10. Henry T. Kurtz, "Battle of Sullivan's Island," in *Amer. Hist. Illus.*, June, 1968, pp. 18–28.

11. Edward M. Riley, "Historic Fort Moultrie," in *S. C. Hist. Mag.*, LI (April, 1950), 63–74.

12. Alexander R. Stoesen, "British Occupation of Charleston, 1779–82," in *S. C. Hist. Mag.*, LXIII (April, 1962), 71–82.

13. Joseph W. Barnwell, "Evacuation of Charleston by the British in 1782," in *S. C. Hist. Mag.*, XI (January, 1910), 1–26.

14. George F. Scheer, "Elusive Swamp Fox," in *American Heritage*, April 1958.

15. Kenneth Roberts, *Oliver Wiswell* (Doubleday, 1940). This novel has one of the most realistic and gripping accounts of the war in South Carolina, especially some of the action at Ninety Six toward the end of the war.

16. Robert D. Bass, "The Campaign of Major Patrick Ferguson," in S. C. Hist. Assoc. *Procdgs.*, 1968, pp. 16–28. King's Mountain, 1780.

17. Lynn Montross, "America's Most Imitated Battle" [Cowpens], in *American Heritage*, April, 1956.

18. Kenneth Roberts, *Battle of Cowpens* (Doubleday, 1957). Useful, but not the best thing Roberts has written.

19. Paul H. Smith, *Loyalists and Redcoats: a Study in British Revolutionary Policy* (U of NC Press, 1964; Paperback, 1968), especially chaps. 7–8.

Section D: SPECIAL TOPICS: (2) BIOGRAPHIES

1. Robert D. Bass, *Green Dragoon* (Holt, 1957). On Tarleton.

2. Don Higginbotham, *Daniel Morgan: Revolutionary Rifleman* (U of NC Press, 1961). Morgan probably is not exactly what some of his enthusiastic followers suggest, but he is no less interesting.

3. Alice N. Waring, *Fighting Elder: Andrew Pickens,*

1739–1817 (U of SC Press, 1962). Fierce Calvinist of the backcountry; Indian fighter and patriot.

4. Anne King Gregorie, *Thomas Sumter* (R. L. Bryan, 1931).

5. D. D. Wallace, *Life of Henry Laurens* (Putnam, 1915; Reprint: Russell, 1967).

6. Robert W. Barnwell, "Rutledge 'the Dictator,' " in *Jour. Sou. Hist.*, VII (May, 1941), 215–24.

7. Richard Barry, *Mr. Rutledge of South Carolina* (Duell, Sloan & Pearce, 1942). While John Rutledge was truly significant, nobody could be quite as significant as he appears in this work of hero worship.

8. Marvin R. Zahniser, *Charles Cotesworth Pinckney: Founding Father* (U of NC Press, 1967).

9. North Callihan, *Daniel Morgan, Ranger of the Revolution* (Holt, Rinehart and Winston, 1961).

10. Theodore Thayer, *Nathanael Greene: Strategist of the American Revolution* (Twayne, 1960). Role played by Greene in South Carolina was perhaps the most crucial of those played by any of the individuals involved.

11. Frances L. Williams, *Plantation Patriot: A Biography of Eliza Lucas Pinckney* (Harcourt, Brace & World, 1967). One of three biographies of this intriguing lady; others are by Nell S. Graydon and by Harriott H. Ravenel.

12. Robert D. Bass has the most popular biographies dealing with the exciting careers of the Patriot guerrillas: *Gamecock* [Thomas Sumter] (Holt, Rinehart & Winston, 1961) ; and *The Swamp Fox* [Francis Marion] (Holt, 1959). Also, above, see *Green Dragoon* [Tarleton].

Section E: CONTEMPORARY DESCRIPTIONS

1. George F. Scheer and Hugh F. Rankin (eds.), *Rebels and Redcoats* (World, 1957; Paperback: Mentor, 1959), chaps. 11, 32–38. Popular and lively.

2. Hugh F. Rankin (ed.), *The American Revolution* (Putnam, 1964; Paperback: Putnam, 1965). A straight survey

type narrative of the Revolution, which Rankin intriguingly put together by using eyewitness accounts. South Carolina events can be followed on pp. 229–313.

3. William T. Bulger (ed.), "Sir Henry Clinton's 'Journal of the Siege of Charleston, 1780,' " in *S. C. Hist. Mag.*, LXVI (July, 1965), 147–74. Includes maps; good to read along with Stoesen article (above).

4. "Col. Robert Gray's Observations on the War in the Carolinas," in *S. C. Hist. Mag.*, XI (July, 1910), 139–59. Good account by a Loyalist.

5. Lee Kennett (ed.), "Charleston in 1778: A French Intelligence Report," in *S. C. Hist. Mag.*, LXVI (April, 1965), 109–11.

6. "Siege of Charleston, 1780," in *Charleston Year Book*, 1897, pp. 341–425. A reprinting of sources, correspondence, statistics.

7. Richard K. Murdoch (ed.), "French Account of the Siege of Charleston, 1780," in *S. C. Hist. Mag.*, LXVII (July, 1966), 138–54.

8. George C. Rogers, Jr. (ed.), "Letters of Charles O'Hara to the Duke of Grafton," in *S. C. Hist. Mag.*, LXV (July, 1964), 158–80.

9. John Drayton, *Memoirs of the American Revolution* (2 vols.; Charleston, 1821; Reprint: Arno, 1960). By a South Carolina governor (1800–02), son of William Henry Drayton, who is much in this. Written from the papers of W. H. Drayton.

10. Banastre Tarleton, *History of the Campaigns of 1780 and 1781* . . . (Dublin, 1787; Reprints: Spartanburg: The Reprint Co., 1967; Arno, 1968). By one of the most colorful and significant Britishers in the conflict.

11. Alexander Chesney, *Journal of . . . a South Carolina Loyalist in the Revolution* (Ohio State U Press 1921).

12. Katharine M. Jones (ed.), *Port Royal Under Six Flags*, Part VII, pp. 119–42.

13. William Moultrie, *Memoirs of the American Revolu-*

tion (2 vols.; New York, 1802; Reprint: 2 vols. in 1; Arno, 1968).

14. W. G. Whilden (ed.), "Extracts from the Diary of Rev. Oliver Hart," in *Charleston Year Book*, 1896, pp. 375–301.

15. Bernard Alexander Uhlendorf (ed.), *The Siege of Charleston . . . Diaries and Letters of Hessian Officers* (U of Mich Press, 1938; Reprint: Arno, 1968).

16. A. S. Salley (ed.), *Colonel William Hill's Memoirs of the Revolution* (Columbia, 1921; Reprint: U of SC Press, 1958).

Section F: OLD ACCOUNTS BY EARLY HISTORIANS

1. Lyman C. Draper, *King's Mountain and Its Heroes* (Cincinnati, 1881; Reprints: Dauber & Pine, 1929; Spartanburg: The Reprint Co., 1967). Based on more careful and thorough research than most early histories.

2. James D. Bailey, *Commanders at King's Mountain* (Gaffney, 1926).

3. Joseph Johnson, *Traditions and Reminiscences of the American Revolution in the South* (Charleston, 1851).

4. David Ramsay, *History of South Carolina*, I, 124–274.

5. David Ramsay, *History of the Revolution in South Carolina* (2 vols.).

6. John Drayton, *Memoirs of the American Revolution*. Limited mostly to South Carolina, and going only "from its commencement to the year 1776, inclusive."

7. Henry Lee, *Memoirs of the War in the South*. (New York, 1812; Reprints: B. Franklin, 1968; Arno, 1969).

8. Henry Lee, Jr., *Campaign of 1781 in the Carolinas* (Philadelphia, 1824; Reprint: Quadrangle, 1962). By son of "Lighthorse Harry" Lee, written as a rebuttal to William Johnson's *Life of Greene*, which he felt had slighted the career of the senior Lee.

9. Alexander Gregg, *History of the Old Cheraws*, chaps. 12–16.

10. Thomas Kirkland and Robert M. Kennedy, *Historic Camden: Colonial and Revolutionary* (Columbia: The State Co., 1926), chaps. 5–14.

11. J. B. O. Landrum, *Colonial and Revolutionary History of Upper South Carolina*, chaps. 12–36.

12. Benson J. Lossing, *Pictorial Field Book of the Revolution* (2 vols.; New York, 1851; Reprint: Spartanburg: The Reprint Co., 1969).

X

Reconstruction and Transition
(1783–1810)

Section A: SPECIAL STUDIES

1. J. Harold Wolfe, *Jeffersonian Democracy in South Carolina* (U of NC Press, 1940; Paperback). A careful, scholarly, thorough political history of this era, tracing not only the beginnings of the Jeffersonians but also discussing the South Carolina Federalists. Includes the Constitutional Convention of 1787, early politics, and state attitudes on the War of 1812 and the background of that conflict.

2. U. B. Phillips, "South Carolina Federalists," in *Amer. Hist. Rev.*, XIV (April, 1909), 529–43; and XIV (July, 1909), 731–45.

3. George C. Rogers, Jr., "South Carolina Ratifies the Federal Constitution," in S. C. Hist. Assoc. *Procdgs.*, 1961, 41–62. Excellent, and blessed with perspective.

4. William A. Schaper, "Sectionalism and Representation in South Carolina," pp. 1–237 in Amer. Hist. Assoc. *Annual Report*, 1900 (New York, 1901); Reprint (as a separate book, with same title: Da Capo Press, 1968). A significant contribution to South Carolina historiography. Deals with divisions within the state down to 1860, but also provides thereby a broader political and economic history of the state than is implied in the title. New edition (1968) has good introduction by Ernest M. Lander, Jr.

5. Charles G. Singer, *South Carolina in the Confederation* (Philadelphia, 1941), especially chaps. 7, 8, 9

Section B: GENERAL HISTORIES OF THE SOUTH

1. John R. Alden, *The First South* (LSU Press, 1961; Paperback; Reprint: Peter Smith, 1968).

2. Thomas P. Abernathy, *The South in the New Nation, 1789–1819* (LSU Press, 1961).

Section C: GENERAL HISTORIES OF SOUTH CAROLINA

1. D. D. Wallace, *History of South Carolina*, II, chaps. 68–71.

2. D. D. Wallace, *South Carolina: A Short History*, chaps. 35–37.

Section D: SPECIAL TOPICS

1. Joseph W. Barnwell (ed.), "Diary of Timothy Ford, 1785–86," in *S. C. Hist. Mag.*, XIII (July, 1912), 132–47; XIII (October, 1912), 181-204. Charming insight into life of the times; one of the best and most readable accounts.

2. D. H. Bacot, "South Carolina Middle Country at the End of the 18th Century," in *So. Atl. Qtrly.*, XXIII (January, 1924), 50–60.

3. D. H. Bacot, "South Carolina Up-Country at the End of the 18th Century," in *Amer. Hist. Rev.*, XXVIII (July, 1923), 682–98. These two articles by Bacot came early in the writing of social history but are still quite useful.

4. Ernest M. Lander, Jr., "South Carolinians at the Philadelphia Convention, 1787," in *S. C. Hist. Mag.*, LVII (July, 1956), 134–55. Shows the important role played by an able group.

5. George C. Rogers, Jr., "Aedanus Burke, Nathanael Greene, Anthony Wayne, and the British Merchants of Charleston," in *S. C. Hist. Mag.*, LXVII (April, 1966), 78–83. Good insight into post-Revolution economic history.

6. Charles C. Nott, *Mystery of the Pinckney Draught: A Study in Constitutional History* (New York, 1908). About the lingering controversy as to whether Charles Pinckney really "wrote the Constitution." Perhaps one should begin

the study of this thorny topic by reading J. Harold Wolfe's monograph (above).

7. Robert C. Cotterill, *The Southern Indians: The Story of the Civilized Tribes before Removal* (U of Okla Press, 1954), *passim*.

8. Charles G. Singer, "Economic, Social, and Political Background," chap. 1 in *South Carolina in the Confederation.* A good summary of the background for this period if one has not previously studied the earlier periods.

9. Charles G. Singer, "Treatment of the Loyalists," chap. 3 in *South Carolina in the Confederation*, pp. 102–25.

10. D. H. Bacot, "Constitutional Progress and the Struggle for Democracy in South Carolina Following the Revolution," in *So. Atl. Qtrly.*, XXIV (January, 1925), 61–72.

11. J. Harold Wolfe, "Roots of Jeffersonian Democracy: With Special Emphasis on South Carolina," in Fletcher M. Green (ed.): *Essays in Southern History* (U of NC Press, 1949; Paperback), pp. 1–15.

12. A. S. Salley, "Origin and Early Development" [of Columbia], in Helen K. Hennig (ed.): *Columbia* (R. L. Bryan, 1936).

13. George S. McCowen, Jr., "Chief Justice John Rutledge and the Jay Treaty," in *S. C. Hist Mag.*, LXII (January, 1961), 10–23. The connection between Rutledge's appointment to the court, the treaty, and partisan political maneuvering.

14. H. T. Cook, *Life and Legacy of David Rogerson Williams* (New York, 1916). Helpful because it concerns one of the most versatile and interesting South Carolinians.

15. Dumas Malone, *Public Life of Thomas Cooper* (Yale U Press, 1926; Reprint: U of SC Press, 1961). Cooper was a revolutionary under many circumstances, not least of all during the period of the increasing importance of the South Carolina College of which he was president. One of the more influential men in the antebellum period.

Section E: CONTEMPORARY DESCRIPTIONS

1. Joseph W. Barnwell (ed.), "Diary of Timothy Ford," in *S. C. Hist. Mag.* XIII (July, 1912), 132–47; and XIII (October, 1912), 181–204.

2. Katharine M. Jones (ed.), "Periclean Age of the Sea Islands," in *Port Royal Under Six Flags*, pp. 143–84.

Section F: OLD ACCOUNTS BY EARLY HISTORIANS

1. John Drayton, *A View of South Carolina, as Respects Her Natural and Civil Concerns.* A governor gives good description of climate, crops, commerce, statistics, and geography. Especially interesting are some views of certain localities.

2. David Ramsay, *History of South Carolina*, II. Ramsay in this second volume departs from his chronological, political history and deals with agriculture, the arts, medical history, and various other topics. He sweeps through state history with each topic but gives a good view of conditions when he was writing in 1808. Especially entertaining and informative is Chap. 10: "Miscellaneous History: Virtues, Vices, Customs, Diversions, &c. of the Inhabitants." This is followed by a series of twenty-one biographical sketches.

XI

War, Boom, and Bust*
(1808–1825)

(*Note*: For economic history of 1825–1860, see Chapter 13, Section D:9.)

Section A: SPECIAL STUDIES

1. Margaret K. Latimer, "South Carolina—A Protagonist of the War of 1812," in *Amer. Hist. Rev.*, LXI (July, 1956), 914–29.

2. Ernest M. Lander, Jr., *Textile Industry in Antebellum South Carolina* (LSU Press, 1969). Comprehensive though small volume, tracing all of the little factories and the beginnings of the modern textile industry stemming from the nucleus at Graniteville.

3. Alfred G. Smith, Jr., *Economic Readjustment of an Old Cotton State: South Carolina 1820–1860* (U of SC Press, 1958; Paperback). Deals with efforts of the state to recover from the "bust" of the 1820's. In doing so, provides excellent economic history of the state.

4. U. B. Phillips, *History of Transportation in the Eastern Cotton Belt to 1860* (New York, 1908; Reprint: Octagon, 1968). A general history, but with much on South Carolina, especially chapters 1 and 2 on roads and canals; chapter 3 on the Charleston to Hamburg Railroad; chapters 4 and 8 on later railroad development.

5. J. Harold Wolfe, *Jeffersonian Democracy in South Carolina*. Thorough on political development, including the coming and the prosecution of the War of 1812 and the role played by South Carolinians therein.

* War of 1812, economic history.

Section B: GENERAL STUDIES IN SOUTHERN HISTORY

1. Thomas P. Abernathy, *The South in the New Nation, 1789–1819* (LSU Press, 1961).

Section C: GENERAL HISTORIES OF SOUTH CAROLINA

1. D. D. Wallace, *History of South Carolina*, II, chaps. 72–74.

2. D. D. Wallace, *South Carolina: A Short History*, chaps. 36, 38, 39.

3. Yates Snowden, *History of South Carolina*, I, chaps. 31–36.

Section D: SPECIAL TOPICS

1. Daniel W. Hollis, "Costly Delusion: Inland Navigation in the South Carolina Piedmont," in S. C. Hist. Assoc. *Procdgs.*, 1968, pp. 29–43.

2. Ernest M. Lander, Jr., "Iron Industry in Ante-Bellum South Carolina," in *Jour. Sou. Hist.*, XX (August, 1954), 337–55.

3. Harriott H. Ravenel, *Charleston*, chaps. 18–19.

4. Robert G. Rhett, *Charleston*, chap. 18.

5. Margaret DesChamps, "Anti-Slavery Presbyterians in the Carolina Piedmont," in S. C. Hist. Assoc. *Procdgs.*, 1954, pp. 6–13.

6. Carl Epting, "Inland Navigation in South Carolina and Traffic on the Columbia Canal," in S. C. Hist. Assoc. *Procdgs.*, 1936, pp. 18–28.

7. E. M. Lander, Jr., "Charleston: Manufacturing Center of the South," in *Jour. Sou. Hist.*, XXVI (August, 1960), 330–51.

8. E. M. Lander, Jr., "Manufacturing in South Carolina, 1815–1860," in *Business Hist. Rev.*, XXVIII (March, 1954), 59–66.

9. E. M. Lander, Jr., "Slave Labor in South Carolina Cotton Mills," in *Jour. Negro Hist.*, XXXVIII (April, 1953), 161–73.

10. Leonard P. Stavisky, "Industrialism in Ante-Bellum Charleston," in *Jour. Negro Hist.*, XXXVI (July, 1951), 302-22.

11. Henry Savage, *Rivers of the Carolinas: The Santee,* chap. 21, on Santee Canal.

Section E: CONTEMPORARY DESCRIPTIONS

1. David Kohn (ed.), *Internal Improvements in South Carolina, 1817-1828* (Washington, 1938). Photographic reproduction of annual reports of state officials, mainly Superintendent of Public Works, involved in road and canal building. Includes maps and extracts from contemporary pamphlets and newspapers. Quite valuable.

2. Robert Mills: *Statistics of South Carolina* (Charleston, 1826; Reprint: University Microfilms). Title not altogether proper; should be "vignettes of South Carolina developments," plus sketches of conditions (and statistics) of each district (county). Both interesting and useful. Subtitle: "including a view of the natural, civil, and military history, general and particular."

3. Robert Mills, "Plans and Progress of Internal Improvements in S. C. . . . ," reprinted in David Kohn (ed.), *Internal Improvements,* pp. 69-92.

4. Lucius G. Moffatt and Joseph M. Carriere (eds.), "A Frenchman Visits Charleston, 1817," in *S. C. Hist. Mag.*, XLIX (July, 1948) 131-54.

5. Lucius V. Bierce, *Travels in the Southland, 1822-23* (Ohio State U Press, 1966). A college student's record. His journal describes part of the upcountry, pp. 73-85.

Numerous travelers' accounts—such as the journals of Francis Asbury—include contemporary observations on the state. This list can be only a sample. For a fully annotated bibliography of such books, see Thomas D. Clark, *Travels in the Old South* (3 vols.; U of Okla Press, 1956-69).

XII

Brinkmanship: Nullification and Its Background (1828–1836)

Section A: SPECIAL STUDIES

1. William W. Freehling, *Prelude to Civil War: the Nullification Controversy in South Carolina, 1816–1836* (Harper & Row, 1965; Paperback: 1968). The best study on the subject; grippingly written. Winner of the Bancroft Prize. Contains some excellent thumbnail biographical sketches.

2. Chauncey S. Boucher, *Nullification Controversy in South Carolina* (Chicago, 1916; Reprints: Russell, 1968; Negro U Press, 1969). Old but still readable and good.

3. David F. Houston, *A Critical Study of Nullification in South Carolina* (Cambridge, Mass., 1896; Reprint: Russell, 1967).

4. John M. Lofton, *Insurrection in South Carolina: The Turbulent World of Denmark Vesey* (Antioch, 1964). The atmosphere in South Carolina at the time of the tariff controversy was influenced by emotions and fears stemming from an 1822 slave insurrection in Charleston led by Vesey.

5. Richard Wade, "The Vesey Plot: a Reconsideration," in *Jour. Sou. Hist.*, XXX (May, 1964), 143–61.

6. Louis Hartz, "South Carolina vs. the United States," in Daniel Aaron (ed.), *America in Crisis* (Knopf, 1952).

Section B: GENERAL STUDIES IN SOUTHERN HISTORY

1. Charles S. Sydnor, *Development of Southern Sectionalism 1819–1847* (LSU Press, 1948; Paperback, 1966).

2. W. J. Cash, *The Mind of the South* (Knopf, 1941; Paperback: Random-Vintage, 1961). One of the most significant studies yet made of the region, by a Carolinian.

Section C: GENERAL HISTORIES OF SOUTH CAROLINA

1. D. D. Wallace, *History of South Carolina*, II, chaps. 75, 76.

2. D. D. Wallace, *South Carolina: A Short History*, chaps. 40, 41.

3. Yates Snowden, *History of South Carolina*, II, chap. 38.

Section D: SPECIAL TOPICS

1. Charles G. Sellers, Jr., "The Travail of Slavery," in *The Southerner as American* (U of NC Press, 1960; Paperback). Concerned with the Southern conscience on slavery.

2. J. M. Lesesne, "Nullification Controversy in Up-Country District," in S. C. Hist. Assoc. *Procdgs.*, 1939, pp. 13–24.

3. Major L. Wilson, " 'Liberty and Union': An Analysis of Three Concepts Involved in the Nullification Controversy," in *Jour. Sou. Hist.*, XXXIII (August, 1967), 331–55.

4. John G. Van Deusen, *Economic Bases for Disunion in South Carolina* (Columbia U Press, 1928).

5. Granville T. Prior, "Charleston Pastimes and Culture During the Nullification Decade, 1822–1832," in S. C. Hist. Assoc. *Procdgs.*, 1940, pp. 36–44.

6. Rosser H. Taylor, "Gentry in Ante-Bellum South Carolina," in *N. C. Hist. Rev.*, XVII (April, 1940), 114–31.

7. George C. Rogers, Jr., "South Carolina Federalists and the Origins of the Nullification Movement," in *S. C. Hist. Mag.*, LXXI (January, 1970), 17–32.

8. Biographies. Too numerous to list here. Exist for nearly all the major figures involved in the nullification episode. The bibliography in Freehling's *Prelude to Civil War* would prove helpful as a guide. All major figures in state history are also in *Dictionary of American Biography*.

XIII

Antebellum Society

Section A: SPECIAL STUDIES

To many readers, this is the most interesting aspect of South Carolina history. Much of it is meshed with Old South historical writing that is not tied to a specific state— an especially rich area of American historiography. On South Carolina, much of the best writing is in periodicals and hence the list below contains many such entries. No truly major social history of South Carolina exists, but the items in this section point the way.

1. Rosser H. Taylor, *Ante-Bellum South Carolina: A Social and Cultural History* (U of NC Press, 1942). Best and only book of this nature; contains something on most of the subsections of this topic (below).

2. J. R. McKissick, "Some Observations of Travelers in South Carolina, 1820–1860," in S. C. Hist. Assoc. *Procdgs.*, 1932, pp. 44–51. Many of the travelogues to which he refers have been recently reprinted.

3. Jack K. Williams, *Vogues in Villainy: Crime and Retribution in Ante-Bellum South Carolina* (U of SC Press, 1959). Although this is basically a monograph on crime and punishment, it reflects much more than that and gives a sharp vignette of antebellum life. Thoroughly readable.

4. George C. Rogers, Jr., *Charleston in the Age of the Pinckneys* (U of Okla Press, 1969). Small but well-grounded in scholarly understanding. Because of restricted space, no mention is being made of the numerous books on Charleston, plantations, architecture, furniture, etc.

5. Lewis E. Atherton, *Southern Country Store, 1800–1860* (LSU Press, 1949).

6. Alfred G. Smith, *Economic Readjustment of an Old Cotton State: South Carolina, 1820–1860* (U of SC Press, 1958). The economic history of the period. Footnotes will beckon the reader to all kinds of inviting paths.

Section B: GENERAL STUDIES IN SOUTHERN HISTORY

1. Charles S. Sydnor, *Development of Southern Sectionalism, 1819–1847* (LSU Press, 1948; Paperback: 1966).

2. Katharine Jones (ed.), *The Plantation South* (Bobbs-Merrill, 1957). Readings from primary sources.

3. Willard Thorp (ed.), *Southern Reader* (Knopf, 1955). Another collection of contemporary source readings.

4. Frank E. Vandiver (ed.), *The Idea of the South: Pursuit of a Central Theme* (U of Chi Press, 1964).

5. Francis B. Simkins, *The Everlasting South* (LSU Press, 1963). Group of essays by distinguished native of South Carolina.

6. U. B. Phillips, *Life and Labor in the Old South* (Little, Brown, 1929; Reprint: Little, Brown 1963; also, Paperback). A classic; largely on plantations and slavery.

7. F. L. Owsley, *Plain Folk of the Old South* (LSU Press, 1949; Reprint: Peter Smith, 1969; Paperback: Quadrangle, 1965). A neglected group who, after all, constituted the majority of the white population.

8. Guion G. Johnson, *Ante-Bellum North Carolina: A Social History* (U of NC Press, 1937). Although the book is not about South Carolina, most of the customs and institutions so well treated in this excellent volume have their counterparts in South Carolina history.

9. Clement Eaton, *Freedom of Thought in the Old South* (Duke U Press, 1940); republished as *Freedom of Thought Struggle in the Old South* (Harper & Row, 1964; Paperback). Traces the shift from liberal views to a "closed society" as the South reacted to criticism of its basic institution.

10. Clement Eaton, *Mind of the Old South* (LSU Press, 1964; rev. ed., 1967; Paperback, 1967).

11. Clement Eaton, *Growth of Southern Civilization, 1790–1860* (Harper & Row, 1961; Paperback: Torchbook). Excellent survey.

12. Clement Eaton, *History of the Old South* (Macmillan, 1949; rev. ed., 1966). First seven chapters (rev. ed.) go through Revolution; chaps. 8–27 are on 1790–1860.

13. Francis B. Simkins: *History of the South* (Knopf, 1953; several later editions). Only good one-volume survey of all Southern history. Chaps. 1–6: Colonial and Revolution; chaps. 7–14, antebellum era; chaps. 15–34, modern period. Unlike most Southern and South Carolina histories, it does not bog down in the early period.

In some respects, one needs to study South Carolina as a part of the Southern story, both political and social. In some areas, South Carolina history can best be seen as part of the whole: for example, there is a paucity of good studies of religion and churches in the state, but recently a number of penetrating books on religion and major denominations in the South have begun to appear. (These examine this basic institution in the context of its society rather than being lists of preachers and statistics, as too often has been the case.)

Section C: GENERAL HISTORIES OF SOUTH CAROLINA

1. D. D. Wallace, *History of South Carolina*, II, chaps. 72, 74, 77; III, chaps. 81–84. Wallace is very good; one could wish he had also undertaken a separate social history.

2. D. D. Wallace, *South Carolina: A Short History*, chaps. 36, 38, 39, 45–47.

Section D: SPECIAL TOPICS: (1) AGRICULTURE

1. J. H. Easterby, "South Carolina Rice Planter as Revealed in the Papers of Robert F. W. Allston" in *Jour. Sou.*

Hist., VII (May, 1941), 160–72. Easterby also has a book
by the same name (U of Chi Press, 1945), which is considered a standard study for understanding this production.

2. Alfred G. Smith, *Economic Readjustment of an Old
Cotton State,* chap. 3.

3. Chalmers S. Murray, *This Is Our Land: Story of the
Agricultural Society of South Carolina* (Carolina Art Assoc.,
1949).

4. Lewis C. Gray, *History of Agriculture in the Southern
United States* (2 vols.: Carnegie Institution, 1933; Reprints:
Peter Smith, 1958; Kelley, 1969). The standard study; not
easy going but essential to one who wants to get at this story.

5. D. C. Heyward, *Seed from Madagascar* (U of NC Press,
1937). History of rice culture.

6. David L. Cohn, *Life and Times of King Cotton* (Oxford
U Press, 1956). Not just on South Carolina.

7. George C. Rogers, Jr., "Georgetown Rice Planters on
the Eve of the Civil War," in *S. C. Hist. Illus.,* I (February,
1970), 24–33.

Section D: SPECIAL TOPICS: (2) SLAVERY AND THE NEGRO

Here again the literature on the subject is voluminous
and becoming more so. There are books on the history of
the Negro, on the history of slavery, on free Negroes, on
slavery in the cities, on slaves' religion, etc.—both general
and state studies. Listed below are a few samples.

1. C. W. Birnie, "Education of the Negro in Charleston
Before the Civil War," in *Jour. Negro Hist.,* XII (January,
1927), 13–21.

2. E. Horace Fitchett, "Status of the Free Negro in
Charleston," in *Jour. Negro Hist.,* XXXII (October, 1947),
430–51.

3. James C. Jackson, "Religious Education of the Negro
in South Carolina Prior to 1850," in *Hist. Mag. of Prot.
Episc. Church,* March, 1967, pp. 35–61.

4. Luther P. Jackson, "Religious Instruction of Negroes,

1830 to 1860, with Special Reference to South Carolina," in *Jour. Negro Hist.*, XV (January, 1930), 72–114.

5. Donald J. Senese, "The Free Negro and the South Carolina Courts, 1790–1860," in *S. C. Hist. Mag.*, LXVIII (July, 1967), 140–53.

6. Howell M. Henry, *Police Control of Slavery in South Carolina* (Emory, Va., 1914; Reprint: Negro U Press, 1968). The law and the regulation of the peculiar institution.

7. Daniel P. Mannix, *Black Cargoes: A History of the Atlantic Slave Trade* (Viking, 1962). An especially unpretty phase of an unpretty history, which has recently been re-examined in this and other books as well as in magazine articles in such periodicals as *American Heritage.*

8. John Lofton, *Insurrection in South Carolina* (Antioch, 1964). The Denmark Vesey rebellion in 1822.

9. T. J. Woofter, *Black Yeomanry: Life on St. Helena Island* (Holt, 1930).

10. Richard C. Wade, *Slavery in the Cities: The South, 1820–1860* (Oxford U Press, 1964; Paperback: 1967).

Section D: SPECIAL TOPICS: (3) EDUCATION

1. J. Perrin Anderson, "Public Education in Ante-Bellum South Carolina," in *S. C. Hist. Assoc. Procdgs.*, 1933, pp. 3–11. "Public education" then did not mean what it does today but rather was a system of "tuition grants" to the indigent, and not much of a system at that.

2. Hugh C. Bailey, "Up-Country Academies of Moses Waddel," in *S. C. Hist. Assoc. Procdgs.*, 1959, pp. 36–43. The most famous and perhaps most successful schoolmaster ever to teach in the state was this Presbyterian minister who had a rural school for boys at Willington (in present McCormick County).

3. Margaret L. Coit, "Moses Waddel: A Light in the Wilderness," in *Ga. Rev.*, V (Spring, 1951), 34–47.

4. Robert S. McCully, "Moses Waddel: Pioneer Pedagogue," in *S. C. Hist. Illus.*, I (February, 1970), 4–10.

5. R. M. Lyon, "Moses Waddel and the Willington Academy," in *N. C. Hist. Rev.* VIII (July, 1931), 284–99.

6. Richard A. Walsh, "The South Carolina Academy, 1800–1811," in S. C. Hist Assoc. *Procdgs.*, 1955, pp. 5–14.

7. Lowell Harrison, "South Carolina's Educational System in 1822," in *S. C. Hist. Mag.*, LI (January, 1950), 1–9.

8. Nita K. Pyburn, "Public School System of Charleston Before 1860," in *S. C. Hist Mag.*, LXI (April, 1960), 86–98.

9. Daniel W. Hollis, "James H. Thornwell and the South Carolina College," in S. C. Hist. Assoc. *Procdgs.*, 1953, pp. 17–36. Thornwell was also distinguished as a Presbyterian divine and was a potent influence in the state.

10. Sarah H. Rembert, "Barhamville: A Columbia Antebellum Girls' School," in *S. C. Hist. Illus.*, I (February, 1970), 44–48.

A number of the colleges in the state have written histories; those written in the past few years are much sounder than some of the earlier efforts. Some of the educators— Thornwell, Cooper, the LeContes—also have been treated by historians.

Section D: SPECIAL TOPICS: (4) CULTURAL AND LITERARY

1. John C. Elem, "Political Newspapers of the S. C. Upcountry, 1850–59: A Compedium," in *S. C. Hist. Mag.*, LXIII (April, 1962), 86–92; LXIII (July, 1962), 158–63. Basic facts; publishers, dates, location of files.

2. Horatio Hughes, "The Elliott Society," in S. C. Hist. Assoc. *Procdgs.*, 1938, pp. 25–31. A group devoted to the study of natural history.

3. Adrienne Koch, "Two Charlestonians in Pursuit of Truth: The Grimké Brothers," in *S. C. Hist. Mag.*, LXIX (July, 1968), 159–70.

4. Frances L. Spain, "Early Libraries in Pendleton," in *S. C. Hist. Mag.*, L (July, 1949), 115–26.

5. S. J. Cohen, *Three Notable Antebellum Magazines of South Carolina* (U of SC Press, 1915).

6. W. J. Mazyck, "Charleston Museum, Its Genesis and Development," in *Charleston Year Book*, 1907, pp. 13–36.

7. Anna W. Rutledge, *Artists in the Life of Charleston* (American Philosophical Society, 1949).

8. Herbert Ravenel Sass, *Outspoken: 150 Years of the News and Courier* (U of SC Press, 1953). Includes history of paper and biographical sketches of those connected with it.

Section D: SPECIAL TOPICS: (5) RECREATION AND ENTERTAINMENT

1. G. T. Prior, "Charleston Pastimes and Culture During the Nullification Decade, 1822–1832," in S. C. Hist. Assoc. *Procdgs.*, 1940, pp. 36–44.

2. William S. Hoole, *Ante-Bellum Charleston Theatre* (U of Ala Press, 1946). This subject, like most others in this booklet, is also covered in broader studies, such as some of the studies of the theater in the South and the theater in colonial America. All travelers' accounts, diaries, and the like would touch on this special topic and others.

3. Lawrence F. Brewster, *Summer Migrations and Resorts of South Carolina Low-Country Planters* (Duke U Press, 1947; Paperback). Entertaining treatment of a subject generally neglected.

4. Sadie S. Patton, *Condensed History of Flat Rock, The Little Charleston of the Mountains* (Asheville: Church Printing Co., 1961).

5. Kenneth F. Marsh, *Historic Flat Rock* (Asheville: Biltmore Press, 1961). Pictures.

6. Lawrence F. Brewster, "Ante-Bellum Planters and Their Means of Transportation," in S. C. Hist. Assoc. *Procdgs.*, 1948, pp. 15–25.

7. Clarence Gohdes (ed.), *Hunting in the Old South: Original Narratives of the Hunters* (LSU Press, 1967).

8. William Elliott, *Carolina Sports by Land and Water* (Charleston, 1846; Reprint: Arno, 1967).

9. Richard B. Harwell, "Hot and Hot Fish Club of All

Saints Parish," in *S. C. Hist. Mag.*, XLVIII (January, 1947), 40–47.

10. W. H. Mills, "The Thoroughbred of South Carolina," in S. C. Hist. Assoc. *Procdgs.*, 1937, pp. 13–24.

Section D: SPECIAL TOPICS: (6) FOLK CULTURE AND LEGENDS

1. John Bennett, *Doctor to the Dead: Grotesque Legends and Folk Tales of Old Charleston* (Rinehart, 1946).

2. Julian S. Bolick, *Return of the Gray Man, and Georgetown Ghosts* (Clinton: Jacobs Brothers Press, 1961).

3. Mary R. Martin, *Charleston Ghosts* (U of SC Press, 1963).

4. DuBose Heyward and Hervey Allen, *Carolina Chansons: Legends of the Low Country* (Macmillan, 1922).

5. Nancy Roberts, *Ghosts of the Carolinas* (Rand McNally, 1962; Paperback).

6. Writers Program, South Carolina, *South Carolina Folk Tales* (Columbia, 1941).

7. Julian S. Bolick, *Ghosts from the Coast: A Collection of Twelve Stories From Georgetown County, South Carolina* (Clinton: Jacobs Brothers Press, 1966).

8. Julian S. Bolick, *Georgetown Ghosts* (Clinton: Jacobs Brothers Press, 1956).

9. Nell S. Graydon, *South Carolina Ghost Tales* (Beaufort, 1969).

Section D: SPECIAL TOPICS: (7) GENERAL AND MISCELLANEOUS

1. J. D. Applewhite, "Some Aspects of Society in Rural South Carolina in 1850," in *N. C. Hist. Rev.*, XXIX (January, 1952), 39–63.

2. Elizabeth W. Pringle, *Chronicles of Chicora Wood, A Southern Plantation Tale* (Scribner's, 1922; Reprint: Boston: Christopher Publishing House, 1940).

3. Elizabeth W. Pringle, *Woman Rice Planter* (Macmillan, 1913; Reprint: Harvard U Press, 1961). (Early editions were published under author's pseudonym, Patience Pen-

nington.) Economic and social conditions in the Georgetown area.

4. Richard Beale Davis, "The Ball Papers, A Pattern of Life in the Low Country, 1800–1825," in *S. C. Hist. Mag.*, LXV (January, 1964), 1–15.

5. Mary Fulton Green, "A Profile of Columbia in 1850," in *S. C. Hist. Mag.*, LXX (April, 1969), 104–21.

6. Rosser H. Taylor, "Gentry in Ante-Bellum South Carolina," in *N. C. Hist. Rev.*, XVII (April, 1940), 114–31. With it, read: Clement Eaton, "Class Differences in the Old South," in *Va. Qtrly. Rev.*, XXXIII (Summer, 1957), 357–70; Paul Buck, "Poor Whites of the Ante-Bellum South," in *Amer. Hist. Rev.*, XXXI (October, 1925), 41–54; and Avery O. Craven, "Poor Whites and Negroes," in *Jour. Negro Hist.*, XV (January, 1930), 14–25.

7. Gilbert P. Voight, "The 'Periclean Age' of Beaufort," in *S. C. Hist. Mag.*, LVIII (October, 1957), 218–23. Will make the modern reader stand in awe and suspect that these really were "the good old days."

8. Jack K. Williams, "Code of Honor in Ante-Bellum South Carolina," in *S. C. Hist. Mag.*, LIV (July, 1953), 113–28. On dueling.

9. Joseph I. Waring, *History of Medicine in South Carolina, 1670–1825* (S. C. Medical Assoc., 1964). Also, Dr. Waring has written *History of Medicine . . . , 1825–1900* (S. C. Medical Assoc., 1967).

10. *Brief History of the South Carolina Medical Association* (S. C. Medical Assoc., 1948). Includes brief sketches of various medical institutions and societies in the state.

11. James W. Patton, "Facets of the South in the 1850's," in *Jour. Sou. Hist.*, XXIII (February, 1957), 3–24.

12. Harvey Wish, *Society and Thought in Early America* (Longmans, Green, 1950), *passim.*

13. Ivan D. Steen, "Charleston in the 1850's: As Described by British Travelers," in *S. C. Hist. Mag.*, LXXI (January, 1970), 36–45.

Section D: SPECIAL TOPICS: (8) ECONOMIC HISTORY, 1825-1860

1. Alfred G. Smith, *Economic Readjustment of an Old Cotton State, 1820-1860* (U of SC Press, 1958; Paperback). The standard study. Chapters: (1) The Old Order Changes; (2) Migration; (3) Agriculture; (4) Manufacturing; (5) Internal Improvements; (6) Banking.

2. Theodore D. Jervey, *Robert Y. Hayne and His Times* (Macmillan, 1909).

3. Samuel M. Derrick, *Centennial History of the South Carolina Railroad* (Columbia: The State Co., 1930).

4. H. Carter Siegling, "The Best Friend of Charleston," in *S. C. Hist. Illus.*, I (February, 1970), 19-23.

5. Harvey T. Cook, *Life and Legacy of David Rogerson Williams* (New York, 1916).

6. Broadus Mitchell, *William Gregg, Factory Master of the Old South* (U of NC Press, 1928; Reprint: Octagon, 1966).

7. Ernest M. Lander, *Textile Industry in Antebellum South Carolina* (LSU Press, 1969).

8. U. B. Phillips, *History of Transportation in the Eastern Cotton Belt to 1860* (Columbia U Press, 1908; Reprint: Octagon, 1968).

9. R. H. Taylor, "Hamburg: an Experiment in Town Promotion," in *N. C. Hist. Rev.*, XI (January, 1934), 20-38.

10. Chauncey S. Boucher, "Ante-Bellum Attitude of South Carolina Toward Manufacturing and Agriculture," in *Washington University* [St. Louis] *Studies*, III (April, 1916), 243-70.

Section E: CONTEMPORARY DESCRIPTIONS

For a guide to travelers' impressions, see the bibliography of Thomas D. Clark, *Travels in the Old South* (3 vols.; U of Okla Press, 1956-69). A veritable gold mine of good reading lies in the accounts listed and annotated there, although many of them are quite scarce and naturally not objective. (Some, not too scarce, are listed in this booklet.) Because of much republishing of such materials, many such records— long lost"—are now becoming readily available.

1. Frederick L. Olmsted, *Journey in the Back Country* (New York, 1860) ; and Frederick L. Olmsted, *Journey in the Seaboard Slave States* (New York, 1856). This Northern traveler is perhaps most often cited by writers, and he is one of the most readable. He also tells much of the "plain folks"—away from the plantation society of alleged "moonlight and roses" flavor. Many editions of these works, or extracts from them, have been reissued, sometimes under different titles. See e.g., F. L. Olmsted, *Slave States Before the Civil War* (ed. by Harvey Wish) (Putnam Capricorn Paperback, 1959), chap. 3; or Olmsted, *Cotton Kingdom* (ed. by Arthur M. Schlesinger) (Knopf, 1953), chaps. 5–6.

2. Katharine Jones (ed.), *Plantation South* (Bobbs-Merrill, 1957), *passim*.

3. J. Rion McKissick, "Some Observations of Travelers in South Carolina, 1820–1860," in S. C. Hist. Assoc. *Procdgs.*, 1932, pp. 44–51.

4. Sidney Walter Martin (ed.), "Ebenezer Kellogg's Visit to Charleston, 1817," in *S. C. Hist. Mag.*, XLIX (January, 1948), 1–14. A diary.

5. Lucius G. Moffatt (ed.), "A Frenchman Visits Charleston, 1817," in *S. C. Hist. Mag.*, XLIX (July, 1948), 131–54.

6. Margaret DesChamps Moore (ed.), "A Northern Professor Winters in Columbia, 1852–53," in *S. C. Hist. Mag.*, LX (October, 1959), 183–92. His letters.

7. John Hammond Moore (ed.), "The Abiel Abbot Journals: A Yankee Preacher in Charleston Society, 1818–1827," in *S. C. Hist. Mag.*, LXVIII (April, 1967), 51–73; LXVIII (July, 1967), 115–39; LXVIII (October, 1967), 232–54.

8. Edwin J. Scott, *Random Collections of a Long Life, 1806–1876* (Columbia, 1884; Reprint: Richland County Historical Society, 1969). Life in Columbia and Lexington.

9. D. E. Huger Smith, *Charlestonian's Recollections, 1846–1913* (Carolina Art Assoc., 1950).

10. Charles Fraser, *Reminiscences of Charleston* (Charleston, 1854; Reprint: Carolina Art Assoc., 1959).

11. Giles J. Patterson, *Journal of a Southern Student, 1846–48* (Vanderbilt U Press, 1944).

12. David Kohn (ed.), *Internal Improvements in South Carolina, 1817–1828* (Washington, 1938).

13. C. G. Parsons, *Inside View of Slavery: or A Tour Among the Planters* (Boston, 1855; Reprints: Argosy, 1969; Negro U Press, 1969).

14. Harvey Wish (ed.), *Slavery in the South: First-Hand Accounts* (Farrar & Straus, 1964; Paperback).

15. Eric L. McKitrick (ed.), *Slavery Defended: The Views of the Old South* (Prentice-Hall, 1963; Paperback, 1963). The opposite view: Theodore Dwight Weld, *American Slavery as It Is: Testimony of a Thousand Witnesses* (New York, 1839; Reprint: Arno, 1968). A collection of contemporary Southerners' comments, gathered and published by a leading antislavery leader.

16. Warren S. Tryon (ed.), *Mirror for Americans* (3 vols.; U of Chi Press, 1952). Vol. II contains extracts from various travelers moving through the Old South.

17. Rev. G. Lewis, *Impressions of America and the American Churches: From Journal of the Rev. G. Lewis* (Edinburgh, 1848; Reprint: Negro U Press, 1968), chaps. 5–6. A preacher from the Free Church of Scotland on a tour here in 1844.

18. Alexander Mackay, *The Western World; or, Travels in the United States in 1846–7* (3 vols.; 2nd ed., London, 1849; Reprint: Negro U Press, 1968), II, chaps. 6, 7.

19. Lillian Foster, *Way-Side Glimpses, North and South* (New York, 1860; Reprint: Negro U Press, 1960), chaps. 12, 13.

20. Cornelia Barrett Ligon, "Legend of the South" [contemporary view of the plantation], in *American Heritage*, June, 1956.

21. Charles Mackay, *Life and Liberty in America: Sketches of a Tour . . . 1857–1858* (New York, 1859).

22. John S. C. Abbott, *South and North: Impressions*

Received During a Trip to Cuba and the South (New York, 1860; Reprint: Negro U Press, 1969).

23. Edward Ingle, *Southern Sidelights* (New York, 1896).

24. Lucius V. Bierce, *Travels in the Southland, 1822–23* (Ohio State U Press, 1966).

25. Nehemicah Adams, *Southside View of Slavery* (Richmond, 1855; Reprint: Negro U Press, 1969).

26. Samuel G. Stoney and Susan S. Bennett (eds.), "Pendleton in the 1830's: Selections from the Langdon Cheves Papers," in *S. C. Hist. Mag.*, XLVII (April, 1946), 69–75.

27. G. W. Featherstonhaugh, *Excursion Through the Slave States* (New York, 1844; Reprint: Negro U Press, 1968), chaps. 43–45.

28. J. S. Buckingham, *Slave States of America* (2 vols.; London, 1842; Reprint: Negro U Press, 1968), I, chaps. 1–6; II, chaps. 1, 2, 7–9.

29. J. Milton Mackie, *From Cape Cod to Dixie and the Tropics* (New York, 1864; Reprint: Negro U Press, 1968), chaps. 7–8. Written before the war.

30. Basil Hall, *Travels in America in the Years 1827 and 1828* (2 vols.; Philadelphia, 1829; Reprint: Johnson, 1970), *passim*.

31. Mrs. A. M. French, *Slavery in South Carolina, and the Ex-slaves; Or, The Port Royal Mission* (New York, 1862; Reprint: Negro U Press, 1968).

32. *Pro-Slavery Argument* (Charleston, 1852; Reprint: Negro U Press, 1968). Essays defending the institution; written by William Harper, James H. Hammond, William Gilmore Simms, and Thomas R. Dew.

XIV

Coming of the Civil War
(1847–1861)

1. Philip M. Hamer, *Secession Movement in South Carolina, 1847–1852* (Allentown, Pa.: Haas & Co., 1918). Monograph on period when state conventions and legislature were lunging at secession but then reluctantly backing away when other Southern states were reluctant to follow.

2. Harold Schultz, *Nationalism and Sectionalism, 1852–1860* (Duke U Press, 1950; Reprint: Da Capo Press, 1969). Another significant book tracing the shifts in temperature of the state.

3. Laura A. White, "The National Democrats of South Carolina, 1852–1860," in *So. At. Qtrly.*, XXVIII (October, 1929), 370–89. The tantalizing story of the "road not taken" under the leadership of moderates headed by James L. Orr, who might have succeeded if circumstances had been a bit different elsewhere. Given enough time, this policy of moderates conceivably might have averted the battle of Fort Sumter.

4. Laura A. White, *Robert Barnwell Rhett, Father of Secession* (Century, 1931; Reprint: Peter Smith, 1965). To offset this fire-eater, the reader may want to read about two who opposed secession: J. P. Carson, *Life, Letters, and Speeches of James L. Petigru* (W. H. Loudermilk & Co., 1920), or Lillian A. Kibler, *Benjamin F. Perry: South Carolina Unionist* (Duke U Press, 1946).

5. Chauncey S. Boucher, *South Carolina and the South on the Eve of Secession, 1852–1860* (Washington U Press, Concord, N. H., 1919).

6. Charles E. Cauthen, *South Carolina Goes to War, 1860–65* (U of NC Press, 1950).

Section B: GENERAL STUDIES IN SOUTHERN HISTORY

1. Avery O. Craven, *Coming of the Civil War* (Scribner's, 1942; Paperback: U of Chi Press, 1957).

2. Avery O. Craven, *Development of Southern Nationalism, 1848–1861* (LSU Press, 1953).

3. Charles W. Ramsdell, "Lincoln and Fort Sumter," in *Jour. Sou. Hist.,* III (August, 1937), 259–88. Classic statement of the theory that Lincoln deliberately maneuvered the South into firing first.

4. Bruce Catton, *Two Roads to Sumter* (McGraw-Hill, 1963).

5. Murat Halstead, "Douglas, Deadlock, and Disunion," in *American Heritage,* August, 1960.

6. Allan Nevins, "The Needless Conflict," in *American Heritage,* August, 1956.

7. David Donald, *Charles Sumner and the Coming of the Civil War* (Knopf, 1960).

8. George Fort Milton, *Eve of Conflict: Stephen A. Douglas and the Needless War* (Houghton-Mifflin, 1934; Reprint: Octagon, 1963).

9. Roy F. Nichols, *Stakes of Power, 1845–1877* (Hill & Wang, 1961; Paperback).

10. George H. Knoles (ed.), *Crisis of the Union, 1860–61* (LSU Press, 1965). Collection of several differing historical interpretations. Of the same nature is Edwin C. Rozwenc (ed.), *Causes of the American Civil War* (Heath, 1961; Paperback); also Kenneth M. Stampp, *And the War Came: The North and the Secession Crisis, 1860–61* (LSU Press, 1950; Paperback: U of Chi Press, 1964).

11. Arnold Whitridge, *No Compromise!* (Farrar, Straus & Cudahy, 1960). Exciting emphasis on the emotional flavor

of the era. Whitridge develops the theme more briefly in "Fanaticism—North and South," in *Va. Qtrly. Rev.*, XXXVIII (Summer, 1962), 494–509.

12. Richard N. Current, *Lincoln and the First Shot* (Lippincott, 1963; Paperback, 1963). One of the best and most fascinating studies of Lincoln's part in the crisis that began the Civil War—a topic which has led to numerous articles and essays—as well as collections of extracts from these various viewpoints about the Fort Sumter crisis.

13. Francis B. Simkins, *History of the South* (Knopf, 1953), chaps. 13, 14; Clement Eaton, *History of the Old South* (Macmillan, 1966), chaps. 23–27.

14. Avery Craven, *Civil War in the Making* (LSU Press, 1959; Paperback, 1968).

Section C: GENERAL HISTORIES OF SOUTH CAROLINA

1. D. D. Wallace, *History of South Carolina*, III, chaps. 85–87.

2. D. D. Wallace, *South Carolina: A Short History*, chaps. 48–50.

Section D: SPECIAL TOPICS

1. W. J. Carnathan, "The Proposal to Reopen the African Slave Trade," in *So. Atl. Qtrly.*, XXV (October, 1926), 410–29.

2. Ronald Takaki, "The Movement to Reopen the African Slave Trade in South Carolina," in *S. C. Hist. Mag.*, LXVI (January, 1965), 38–54.

3. Jack K. Williams, "Southern Movement to Reopen the African Slave Trade, 1954–1860: A Factor in Secession," in *S. C. Hist. Assoc. Procdgs.*, 1960, pp. 23–31.

4. T. W. Rogers, "Great Population Exodus from South Carolina, 1850–1860," in *S. C. Hist. Mag.*, LXVIII (January, 1967), 14–21.

5. N. W. Stephenson, "Southern Nationalism in South Carolina in 1851," in *Amer. Hist. Rev.*, XXXVI (January, 1931), 314–35.

6. A. L. Venable, "The Conflict between the Douglas and Yancey Forces in the Charleston Convention," in *Jour. Sou. Hist.*, VIII (May, 1942), 226–41.

7. Laura A. White, "The Fate of Calhoun's Sovereign Convention in South Carolina," in *Amer. Hist. Rev.*, XXXIV (July, 1929), 757–71.

8. Carl N. Degler, "There Was Another South," in *American Heritage*, August, 1960. Degler argues that many in the South were really "out of step" with the hotheads.

9. Ralph A. Wooster, *The People in Power: Courthouse and Statehouse in the Lower South, 1850–1860* (U of Tenn Press, 1969). An analysis, with many statistics, outlining the nature and makeup of local and state government in this period.

XV

Civil War
(1861–1865)

Section A: SPECIAL STUDIES

1. Charles E. Cauthen, *South Carolina Goes to War, 1860–1865* (U of NC Press, 1950). The only really good study on this major topic. The Civil War "has been written to death" but the separate story of South Carolina has not been generally treated.

2. Robert Carse, *Department of the South: Hilton Head Island in the Civil War* (Columbia: The State Printing Co., 1961).

3. John Barrett, *Sherman's March Through the Carolinas* (U of NC Press, 1956). The definitive and readable military history.

4. Willie Lee Rose, *Rehearsal for Reconstruction: The Port Royal Experiment* (Bobbs-Merrill, 1964; Paperback: Vintage). Winner of Allan Nevins History Prize. Able scholarship dealing with the sea islands which were occupied by Union forces throughout the war as a beachhead and also as an area for experiment as implied in the title.

Section B: GENERAL STUDIES IN SOUTHERN HISTORY
(*Note:* Military histories excluded.)

1. James G. Randall and David Donald, *Civil War and Reconstruction* (2nd ed.; Heath, 1961), chaps. 1–30. Probably best single-volume study touching all aspects of the period.

2. E. Merton Coulter, *Confederate States of America* (LSU Press, 1950).

3. Bell I. Wiley, *Road to Appomattox* (Memphis St Coll Press, 1956; Paperback: Atheneum, 1968).

4. Charles P. Roland, *The Confederacy* (U of Chi Press, 1960; Paperback). Small, but shows good scholarship.

5. N. W. Stephenson, *Day of the Confederacy* (Yale U Press, 1920; Reprint: U.S. Pubs, 1968). In the popular *Yale Chronicles* series.

6. Charles W. Ramsdell, *Behind the Line in the Confederacy* (LSU Press, 1944; Reprint: 1969). Phase of history that has been neglected for the military campaigns.

7. Bell I. Wiley, *The Plain People of the Confederacy* (LSU Press, 1943; Reprint: Peter Smith, 1967; Paperback: Quadrangle, 1963). A group who have been most neglected, despite their large numbers.

8. Bell I. Wiley, *Southern Negroes, 1861–1865* (Yale U Press, 1938; Reprint: Rinehart, 1953; Paperback: Yale U Press, 1965).

9. Francis B. Simkins, *History of the South* (Knopf, 1953), chap. 15.

Section C: GENERAL HISTORIES OF SOUTH CAROLINA

1. D. D. Wallace, *History of South Carolina*, III, chaps. 88–90.

2. D. D. Wallace, *South Carolina: A Short History*, chaps. 51, 52.

3. Yates Snowden, *History of South Carolina*, II, chaps. 43–55.

Section D: SPECIAL TOPICS

1. John G. Barrett, "Sherman and Total War in the Carolinas," in *N. C. Hist. Rev.*, XXXVII (July, 1960), 367–81.

2. John C. Ellen, "Richard Yeadon, Confederate Patriot," in S. C. Hist. Assoc. *Procdgs.*, 1960, pp. 32–43.

3. Shelby Foote, "Du Pont Storms Charleston," in *American Heritage*, June, 1963. Readable account of mid-war attacks on Fort Sumter and nearby areas.

4. William S. Hoole, "Charleston Theatricals during the Tragic Decade, 1860–1869," in *Jour. Sou. Hist.* XI (November, 1945), 538–47.

5. Saunders Redding, "Tonight for Freedom," in *American Heritage*, June 1958. Negroes on Morris Island.

6. Francis B. Simkins and James S. Patton, "Work of Southern Women among the Sick and Wounded of the Confederate Army," in *Jour. Sou. Hist.*, I (November, 1935), 475–96.

7. Leah Townsend, "Confederate Gunboat *Peedee*," in *S. C. Hist. Mag.*, LX (April, 1959), 66–73.

8. Thornwell Jacobs, *Red Lanterns on St. Michaels* (Dutton, 1940). Historical novel.

9. Roy Meredith, *Storm Over Sumter* (Simon & Schuster, 1957).

10. W. A. Swanberg, *First Blood: Fort Sumter* (Scribner's, 1957).

Section E: CONTEMPORARY DESCRIPTIONS

1. Martin Abbott and Elmer L. Puryear (eds.), "Beleaguered Charleston: Letters from the City, 1860–1864," in *S. C. Hist. Mag.*, LXI (April, 1960), 61–74; LXI (July, 1960), 164–75; LXI (October, 1960), 210–18. Informative and lively observations of life in the city by Charles K. Rogers.

2. Clement Eaton (ed.), "Diary of an Officer in Sherman's Army Marching Through the Carolinas," in *Jour. Sou. Hist.*, IX (May, 1943), 238–54.

3. P. J. Staudenraus (ed.), "Occupied Beaufort, 1863: A War Correspondent's View," in *S. C. Hist. Mag.*, LXIV (July, 1963), 136–44. Entertaining descriptions by a special correspondent of the Sacramento *Daily Union*.

4. "Union Soldier at Fort Sumter, 1860–61," in *S. C. Hist. Mag.*, LXVII (April, 1966), 99–104. Two Letters.

5. William H. Russell, *My Diary North and South* (Boston, 1863; Reprint: Harper, 1954), chaps. 10–21. Views of an English newspaper correspondent, early in the war.

6. Earl S. Miers (ed.), *When the World Ended* (Oxford U Press, 1957). The diary of Emma LeConte on the burning of Columbia, 1865.

7. Katharine M. Jones (ed.), *Port Royal Under Six Flags*, Parts 9–11.

8. Katharine M. Jones (ed.), *When Sherman Came: Southern Women and the "Great March"* (Bobbs-Merrill, 1964), pp. 109–256. Feminine observations of the event.

XVI

First Reconstruction*
(1865–1868)

* Sometimes called "Presidential Reconstruction" or "White Reconstruction."

thinks it should be required reading for both Northerners and Southerners.

Section C: GENERAL HISTORIES OF SOUTH CAROLINA

1. D. D. Wallace, *History of South Carolina*, III, chaps. 91–92.

2. D. D. Wallace, *South Carolina: A Short History*, chap. 53.

3. Ernest M. Lander, *History of South Carolina, 1865–1960* (U of SC Press, 1970), chap. 1. A small volume that does not claim to be the last word. Nevertheless, this survey serves a real need since thus far much of the material has not been treated at all elsewhere.

Section D: SPECIAL TOPICS

1. Martin Abbott, "Freedman's Bureau and Negro Schooling in South Carolina," in *S. C. Hist. Mag.*, LVII (April, 1956), 65–81.

2. Hermine M. Baumhofer, "Economic Changes in St. Helena's Parish, 1860–1870," in *S. C. Hist. Mag.*, L (January, 1949), 1–13.

3. F. B. Simkins, "Problems of South Carolina Agriculture after the Civil War," in *N. C. Hist. Rev.*, VII (January, 1930), 46–77; VII (April, 1930), 192–219.

4. J. H. Wolfe, "South Carolina Constitution of 1865 as a Democratic Document," in S. C. Hist. Assoc. *Procdgs.*, 1942, pp. 18–29.

5. Robert H. Woody, "Some Aspects of the Economic Condition of South Carolina after the Civil War," in *N. C. Hist. Rev.*, VII (July, 1930), 346–64.

6. J. P. Hollis, *Early Period of Reconstruction in South Carolina* (Johns Hopkins Press, 1905; Reprint: Da Capo, 1970).

Section E: CONTEMPORARY DESCRIPTIONS

1. Harvey Wish (ed.), *Reconstruction in the South, 1865–1877: First Hand Accounts* (Farrar & Straus, 1965; Paper-

back). An entertaining collection of many extracts from travelers' accounts. Especially useful are the reports of Northerners who came South in 1865–66 and reported on the status of the region and their opinion of its loyalty to the Union.

2. John R. Dennett, *The South As It Is, 1865–66* (Viking, 1965; Paperback). One of the Northern travelers. See especially, pp. 178–263.

3. Whitelaw Reid, *After the War: A Tour of Southern States, 1865–1866* (Cincinnati, 1866; Reprint: Peter Smith, 1965; Paperback: Torchbook, 1965), chaps. 7–12.

4. John T. Trowbridge, *The Desolate South 1865–66* (Hartford, 1866; Reprint: Duell, Sloan & Pearce, 1956), chaps. 34–37.

5. Sidney Andrews, *The South Since the War* (Boston, 1866; Reprint: Arno, 1969). Also, an extract from this describing South Carolina is in Warren S. Tryon (ed.), *Mirror for Americans* (3 vols.; U of Chi Press, 1952), II, 442–466.

6. David Macrae, *The Americans at Home* (2 vols.; Edinburgh, 1870), I, chaps. 28, 29.

7. Robert Somers, *Southern States Since the War: 1870–71* (London, 1871; Reprint: U of Ala Press, 1965), chaps. 6–10 in 1965 reprint edition.

8. Myrta L. Avary, *Dixie After the War* [on 1865–1877] (New York, 1906; Reprints: Houghton, 1937; Da Capo Press, 1970), *passim*.

XVII

Radical Reconstruction
(1868–1877)

Note: Although a tremendous amount of material exists on South Carolina during Reconstruction, the titles suggested below will be few. Persons not recently in the academic world would be well advised before touching this thorny topic to investigate what has been going on among historians in recent years as they keep studying this controversial era. Because of this commotion, readers will not find Claude Bowers' *Tragic Era* listed here, perhaps to their surprise. To understand these changes in views about the period, one would do well to read at least one of the following:

1. Bernard A. Weisberger, "The Dark and Bloody Ground of Reconstruction Historiography," in *Jour. Sou. Hist.*, XXV (November, 1959), 427–47.

2. T. Harry Williams, "Analysis of Some Reconstruction Attitudes," in *Jour. Sou. Hist.*, XII (November, 1946), 469–86.

3. Francis B. Simkins, "New Viewpoints of Southern Reconstruction," in *Jour. Sou. Hist.*, V (February, 1939), 49–61.

4. Neill W. Macaulay, "South Carolina Reconstruction Historiography," in *S. C. Hist. Mag.*, LXV (January, 1964), 20–32.

Section A: SPECIAL STUDIES

1. Francis B. Simkins and Robert H. Woody, *South Caro-

lina During Reconstruction (U of NC Press, 1932; Reprint: Peter Smith, 1966). Still good; readable.

2. Joel Williamson, *After Slavery: The Negro in South Carolina During Reconstruction, 1861–1877* (U of NC Press, 1965; Paperback: 1969). A major revision, the result of impressive new research. Takes issue with C. Vann Woodward's thesis that has had such an impact since the 1950's. A brilliant and provocative book.

3. Hampton Jarrell, *Wade Hampton and the Negro* (U of SC Press, 1949). Convincingly makes the argument that Hampton was a moderate on race relations (certainly for his day) and opposed the "shotgun policy" of terror and intimidation that was used by some of his supporters of 1876. Argument has continued as to which phase of the campaign tactics determined the outcome.

Section B: GENERAL STUDIES IN SOUTHERN HISTORY

(None of these volumes has special chapters on South Carolina, but the state usually gets much attention in any Reconstruction history.)

1. James G. Randall and David Donald, *Civil War and Reconstruction* (2nd ed.; 1961), chaps. 31–39.

2. E. M. Coulter, *The South During Reconstruction* (LSU Press, 1947). Volume in the distinguished *History of the South* series, but has been criticized by some of the recent scholars for not having taken advantage of the new scholarship and for not being as objective as most volumes in that series.

3. Kenneth M. Stampp, *Era of Reconstruction, 1865–1877* (Knopf, 1965; Paperback: Vintage). Author is one of the most distinguished young contemporary scholars, although some South Carolinians would dispute his viewpoint.

4. Richard N. Current, *Reconstruction, 1865–1877* (Prentice-Hall, 1965; Paperback: Vintage).

5. Thomas D. Clark and Albert D. Kirwan, *The South Since Appomattox: A Century of Regional Change* (Oxford

U Press, 1967), chaps. 1, 2. Thought-provoking judgments accompany this narrative which somehow manages to be different from the two other general surveys. See them also: F. B. Simkins, *History of the South* (Knopf, 1953), chaps. 16–19 (an excellent story of Reconstruction, by an author who specialized in the story of South Carolina); and John S. Ezell, *The South Since 1865* (Macmillan, 1963), chaps. 3–5.

Section C: GENERAL HISTORIES OF SOUTH CAROLINA

1. D. D. Wallace, *History of South Carolina*, III, chaps. 91–97.

2. D. D. Wallace, *South Carolina: A Short History*, chaps. 53–56.

3. E. M. Lander, *History of South Carolina, 1865–1960*, chap. 1.

Section D: SPECIAL TOPICS

1. Edgar W. Knight, "Reconstruction in Education in South Carolina," in *So. Atl. Qtrly.*, XVIII (October, 1919), 350–64; XIX (January, 1920), 55–66.

2. Herbert Shapiro, "Ku Klux Klan During Reconstruction: The South Carolina Episode," in *Jour. Negro Hist.*, XLIX (January, 1964), 34–55; also, F. B. Simkins, "The Ku Klux Klan in South Carolina, 1868–1871," in *Jour. Negro Hist.*, XII (October, 1927), 606–47.

3. F. B. Simkins, "Election of 1876 in South Carolina," in *So. Atl. Qtrly.*, XXI (July, 1922), 225–40; XXI (October, 1922), 335–51.

4. F. B. Simkins, "White Methodism in South Carolina During Reconstruction," in *N. C. Hist. Rev.*, V (January, 1928), 35–64.

5. Robert H. Woody, "Franklin J. Moses, Jr.," in *N. C. Hist. Rev.*, X (April, 1933), 111–32. The most intriguing, but not the most admirable character of the era.

6. Herbert L. Swint, *Northern Teacher in the South* (Vanderbilt U Press, 1941; Reprint: Octagon, 1966).

7. Francis Griswold, *Sea Island Lady* (W. Morrow, 1939; Reprint, 1942). Historical novel.

8. Robert G. Rhett, *Charleston*, chaps. 25–27.

9. Martin Abbott, *Freedmen's Bureau in South Carolina, 1865–1872* (U of NC Press, 1967). An interesting book that provides a convincing reinterpretation of the traditional views of this agency in the state.

10. Manly W. Wellman, *Giant in Gray: A Biography of Wade Hampton of South Carolina* (Scribner's, 1949). Hampton is still awaiting a definitive biography. This one is long on romance and military glory, but less satisfactory on his postwar career, perhaps his more important period.

Section E: CONTEMPORARY DESCRIPTIONS

1. Katharine C. Jones (ed.), *Port Royal Under Six Flags*, Part 10.

2. Harvey Wish (ed.), *Reconstruction in the South, 1865–1877: First-Hand Accounts by Northerners and Southerners* (Farrar, Straus, and Giroux, 1965; Paperback), *passim*.

3. Louis F. Post, "A Carpet-Bagger in South Carolina," in *Jour. Negro Hist.*, X (January, 1925), 10–29.

4. John William DeForest, *Union Officer in the Reconstruction* (Yale U Press, 1948; Reprint: Shoe String Press, 1968). One of the best items in this abbreviated list. DeForest was a Northerner, a novelist, who was stationed in the Greenville-Pickens area to do relief work with the Freedmen's Bureau.

5. James S. Pike, *The Prostrate State* (New York, 1874; Reprint: Loring & Mussey, 1935; Paperback: Torchbook, 1968). Contemporary work of a Northern journalist, cited in many footnotes of those writing about Reconstruction during the "Lost Cause" cult. In recent years, his credibility has been seriously questioned.

Section F: OLD ACCOUNTS BY EARLY HISTORIANS

Note: These are hardly ancient writings, but generally

they have been supplanted, revised, or rebutted by trained scholars of the last few years.

1. John S. Reynolds, *Reconstruction in South Carolina* (Columbia: The State Co., 1905; Reprint: Negro U Press, 1969).

2. Alfred B. Williams, *Hampton and His Red Shirts* (Walker, Evans & Cogswell, 1935). In this, Hampton is the hero—almost a saint. By a contemporary observer, a journalist.

3. William A. Sheppard, *Red Shirts Remembered* (Atlanta: Ruralist Press, 1940). In this, Hampton is anything but a hero. A strident defense of Martin W. Gary, and very anti-Hampton.

4. A. A. Taylor, *The Negro in South Carolina during Reconstruction* (Washington, 1924; Reprints: AMS, 1969; Russell, 1969). Appeared first in *Jour. Negro Hist.*, IX (July, 1924), 241–364; IX (October, 1924), 381–569.

5. Laura J. Webster, *Operation of the Freedmen's Bureau in South Carolina* (Northampton, Mass.: Smith College, 1916; Reprint: Russell, 1969).

6. Edward L. Wells, *Hampton and Reconstruction* (Columbia: The State Co., 1907).

XVIII

Bourbon Era
(1877–1890)

Section A: SPECIAL STUDIES

1. William J. Cooper, *Conservative Regime: South Carolina, 1877–1890* (Johns Hopkins Press, 1968). Prior to publication of this book, this era had been largely neglected. This study limited mainly to political history.

2. George B. Tindall, *South Carolina Negroes, 1877–1890* (U of SC Press, 1952; Paperback: LSU Press, 1966). Much that is original and valuable is in this admirable study. Listed here as a major study because it is even broader than its title and serves partially as a social history of the period.

Section B: GENERAL STUDIES IN SOUTHERN HISTORY

1. C. Vann Woodward, *Origins of the New South, 1877–1913* (LSU Press, 1951; Paperback, 1966). One of the most significant books published on Southern history in the last several decades because it broke so much ground about a period not studied much but which may have been more formative on Southern customs and mores than have some of the more dramatic eras.

2. Nash K. Burger and J. K. Bettersworth, "Redeeming Arm: Wade Hampton," chap. 8 of *South of Appomattox* (Harcourt, Brace, and World, 1959), pp. 236–72. A book on the role of ex-Confederate leaders during the Bourbon era.

3. Francis B. Simkins, *History of the South*, chaps. 21, 22.

4. John S. Ezell, *The South Since 1865*, chap. 6. Most of

the chapters in this excellent book are topical (e.g., "Southern Agriculture, 1865–1930") and hence do not lend themselves to the chronological divisions of this booklet.

5. Clement Eaton, *Waning of the Old South Civilization, 1860–1880's* (U of Ga Press, 1968; Paperbacks: Pegasus, 1969; U of Calif Press, 1969).

Section C: GENERAL HISTORIES OF SOUTH CAROLINA

1. D. D. Wallace, *History of South Carolina*, III, chaps. 98, 99.

2. D. D. Wallace, *South Carolina: A Short History*, chap. 57.

3. E. M. Lander, *History of South Carolina, 1865–1960*, chap. 2. This book, like that by Ezell (above), is mainly in topical chapters—for example, South Carolina "Education and Religion, 1865–1941"—which do not fit neatly into the arrangement of this booklet.

Section D: SPECIAL TOPICS

1. Elizabeth Davidson, "Early Development of Public Opinion against Southern Child Labor," in *N. C. Hist. Rev.*, XIV (July, 1937), 230–50.

2. Broadus Mitchell, "Some Southern Industrialists," in *Va. Qtrly. Rev.*, V (January, 1929), 103–14.

3. Broadus Mitchell, *Rise of the Cotton Mills in the South* (Johns Hopkins Press, 1921; Reprints: Peter Smith, 1966; Da Capo (2nd ed.), 1968). Not limited to South Carolina, but the period 1880–1910 marks the beginning of the industrial revolution in the area.

4. William H. Simpson, *Life in Mill Communities* (Presbyterian College Press, Clinton, S. C., 1943).

5. Thomas F. Parker, "The South Carolina Cotton Mill— A Manufacturer's View," in *So. Atl. Qtrly.*, VIII (October, 1909), 328–37.

6. T. F. Parker, "The South Carolina Cotton Mill Village: A Manufacturer's View," in *So. Atl. Qtrly.*, IX (October, 1910), 349–57.

7. William E. Woodward, "A Cotton Mill Village in the 1880's," chap. 10 in *The Way Our People Lived* (Dutton, 1944; Reprint: Liveright, 1963; Paperbacks: Washington Square Press, 1968; Pocket Books, 1957). The village: Graniteville.

8. J. H. Easterby, "Granger Movement in S. C.," in S. C. Hist. Assoc. *Procdgs*, 1931, pp. 21–32.

9. F. B. Simkins, *Pitchfork Ben Tillman* (LSU Press, 1944; Reprint: Peter Smith, 1964; Paperback: LSU Press, 1967), chap. 6.

10. S. Frank Logan, "Francis W. Dawson," in S. C. Hist. Assoc. *Procdgs.*, 1952, pp. 13–28. The editor of *The News & Courier* until 1889.

11. Francis B. Simkins, "The Negro in S. C. Law Since 1865," in *So. Atl. Qtrly.*, XX (January, 1921), 61–71; XX (April, 1921), 165–177.

12. George B. Tindall, "Campaign for the Disfranchisement of Negroes in South Carolina," in *Jour. Sou. Hist.*, XV (May, 1949), 212–34.

13. George B. Tindall, "The Liberian Exodus of 1878," in *S. C. Hist. Mag.*, LIII (July, 1952), 133–45. The story of an expedition to take Carolina Negroes back to Africa. Also in his book *South Carolina Negroes* (above).

14. Albert D. Oliphant, *Evolution of the Penal System in South Carolina from 1866 to 1916* (Columbia: The State Co., 1916). In connection with this, see Fletcher M. Green, "Some Aspects of the Convict Lease System in the Southern States," chap. 7 in Fletcher M. Green (ed.), *Essays in Southern History* (U of NC Press, 1949; Paperback), pp. 112–23.

15. James W. Patto, "Republican Party in South Carolina, 1876–1910," chap. 6 in Fletcher M. Green (ed.), *Essays in Southern History* (U of NC Press, 1949; Paperback), pp. 91–111.

16. George L. Simpson, *The Cokers of Carolina* (U of NC Press, 1956).

17. Carol K. Rothrock Bleser, *The Promised Land: His-

tory of the South Carolina Land Commission, 1869–1890
(U of SC Press, 1969).

18. Joseph I. Waring, *History of Medicine in South Carolina, 1825–1900* (S. C. Medical Assoc., 1967).

Section E: CONTEMPORARY DESCRIPTION

1. Sir George Campbell, *White and Black: The Outcome of a Visit to the United States* (New York, 1879; Reprint: Negro U Press, 1969), pp. 312–46. A description of the state just after Hampton had taken over following the disputed election of 1876.

XIX

Agrarian Revolt and Tillmanism
(1890–1900)

Section A: SPECIAL STUDIES

1. Francis B. Simkins, *Pitchfork Ben Tillman, South Carolinian* (LSU Press, 1944; Reprint: Peter Smith, 1964; Paperback: LSU Press, 1967). One of the major biographies in South Carolina historiography. Objective in general and quite readable. Valuable because it covers so many years about which so little has been published.

2. Francis B. Simkins, *Tillman Movement in South Carolina* (Duke U Press, 1926).

Section B: GENERAL STUDIES IN SOUTHERN HISTORY

1. C. Vann Woodward, *Origins of the New South, 1877–1913* (LSU Press, 1951; Paperback, 1966), chaps. 9–13.

2. John S. Ezell, *The South Since 1865,* chap. 9.

3. Thomas D. Clark and Albert D. Kirwan, *The South Since Appomattox* (Oxford U Press, 1967), chap. 3.

4. Francis B. Simkins, *History of the South,* chap. 22.

5. Daniel Robinson, "From Tillman to Long: Some Striking Leaders of the Rural South," in *Jour. Sou. Hist.,* III (August, 1937), 289–310.

Section C: GENERAL HISTORIES OF SOUTH CAROLINA

1. D. D. Wallace, *History of South Carolina,* III, chaps. 100–104.

2. D. D. Wallace, *South Carolina: A Short History,* chaps 58, 59.

3. E. M. Lander, *History of South Carolina, 1865–1960*, chaps. 2, 5.

Section D: SPECIAL TOPICS

1. Ellen A. Hendricks, "South Carolina Dispensary System," in *N. C. Hist. Rev.*, XXII (April, 1945), 176–97; XXII (July, 1945), 320–49. Also, F. B. Simkins, "South Carolina Dispensary," in *So. Atl. Qtrly.*, XXV (January, 1926), 13–24.

2. W. A. Mabry, "Ben Tillman Disfranchised the Negro," in *So. Atl. Qtrly.*, XXXVII (April, 1938), 170–83. Also, on this topic, Albert N. Sanders, "Jim Crow Comes to South Carolina," in S. C. Hist. Assoc. *Procdgs.*, 1966, pp. 27–39.

3. C. Vann Woodward, *The Strange Career of Jim Crow* (Oxford U Press, 1955; Revised, 1957, 1966; Paperback: 1966), *passim*.

4. Gus G. Williamson, Jr., "South Carolina Cotton Mills and the Tillman Movement," in S. C. Hist. Assoc. *Procdgs.*, 1949, pp. 36–49.

5. F. B. Simkins, "Ben Tillman's View of the Negro," in *Jour. Sou. Hist.*, III (May, 1937), 161–74. Tillman is much involved because of the 1895 Constitutional Convention.

6. Phillips Russell, "Plowboy from Edgefield," in *Va. Qtrly. Rev.*, VIII (October, 1932), 514–29.

7. George B. Tindall, *South Carolina Negroes, 1877–1900* (U of SC Press, 1952; Paperback: LSU Press, 1966). A very significant and useful book. See chap. 5 concerning Negro disfranchisement by the 1895 Constitution.

XX

New Era Begins to Dawn
(1900–1940)

So little has been written about the twentieth century that it is difficult to classify or yet judge what is most significant. In addition, the recent history of the state does not lend itself to neat periods, such as "The Bourbon Period." For example, was 1900–1917 the "Era of Bleaseism" or the "Era of Progressivism"? Is there anything distinctively different about the 1920's? And the "Era of Depression" was hardly a purely South Carolina phenomenon. Much of the history of the twentieth century is yet to be written, and some of it—already written—has not yet seen printer's ink.

Section A: SPECIAL STUDIES

Although there are a number of unpublished dissertations on various aspects of twentieth-century South Carolina, thus far no published work can be considered sufficiently "standard" to be included in this topic or category, which has been included in all previous chapters.

Section B: GENERAL STUDIES IN SOUTHERN HISTORY

1. Francis B. Simkins, *History of the South,* chaps. 23–31.
2. John S. Ezell, *The South Since 1865,* chaps. 10–21.
3. Thomas D. Clark and Albert D. Kirwan, *The South Since Appomattox,* chaps. 5–14.
4. Thomas D. Clark, *The Emerging South* (Oxford U

Press, 1961; Revised, 1968; Paperback, 1968). Covers the period since 1920.

5. C. Vann Woodward, *Origins of the New South, 1877–1913*, chaps. 11–17.

6. George B. Tindall, *Emergence of the New South 1913–1945* (LSU Press, 1967). Like Woodward's *Origins of the New South*, Tindall's 807-page volume marks a significant milestone in Southern historical writing. Naturally not limited to South Carolina, both of these studies give much information on the state. Woodward is a native of Georgia; Tindall is a native of Greenville.

Section C: GENERAL HISTORIES OF SOUTH CAROLINA

1. D. D. Wallace, *History of South Carolina*, III, chaps. 105–11.

2. D. D. Wallace, *South Carolina: A Short History*, chaps. 60–65.

3. E. M. Lander, *History of South Carolina, 1865–1960*, chaps. 3–6.

Section D: SPECIAL TOPICS

1. Ronald D. Burnside, "Racism in the Administration of Gov. Cole Blease," in S. C. Hist. Assoc. *Procdgs.*, 1964, pp. 43–57.

2. Clarence N. Stone, "Bleaseism and the 1912 Election in South Carolina," in *N. C. Hist. Rev.*, XL (January, 1963), 54–74.

3. Oscar L. Warr, "Mr. Blease of South Carolina," in *American Mercury*, XVI (January, 1929), 25–32.

4. F. B. Simkins, "Blease," chap. 32 in *Pitchfork Ben Tillman*.

5. Daniel M. Robinson, "From Tillman to Long: Some Striking Leaders of the Rural South," in *Jour. Sou. Hist.*, III (August, 1937), 289–310. A summary of the "Dixie demagogues" about whom much has been written in recent decades—some of it rather entertaining.

6. John Hammond Moore, "South Carolina's Reaction to the Photoplay 'Birth of a Nation,' " in S. C. Hist. Assoc. *Procdgs.*, 1963, pp. 30–40.

7. W. Ernest Douglas, "Retreat from Conservatism: The Old Lady of Broad Street [*The News & Courier*] Embraces Jim Crow," in S. C. Hist. Assoc. *Procdgs.*, 1958, pp. 3–11. On this, also see C. Vann Woodward, *The Strange Career of Jim Crow.*

8. Daniel W. Hollis, "Samuel Chiles Mitchell, Social Reformer in Blease's South Carolina," in *S. C. Hist. Mag.*, LXX (January, 1969), 20–37. President of the University (1908–13), a Progressive who resigned after severe attacks by Governor Blease.

9. J. H. Eleazer, *A Dutch Fork Farm Boy* (U of SC Press, 1952).

10. Ben Robertson, *Red Hills and Cotton: An Upcountry Memory* (Knopf, 1942; Reprint: U of SC Press, 1963). Autobiographical. Robertson, who became a distinguished journalist, describes life as it really was in the South in the early 20th century.

11. John A. Rice, *I Came Out of the Eighteenth Century* (Harper, 1942). Another autobiography; in this case, by an educator who grew up in South Carolina Methodist parsonages. The first three chapters give the flavor of South Carolina at the end of the 19th and beginning of the 20th century.

12. James F. Byrnes, *All in One Lifetime* (Harper & Row, 1958). Autobiography by the most famous politician produced in the state in recent years.

13. George L. Simpson, *The Cokers of Carolina* (U of NC Press, 1956).

14. William H. Simpson, *Life in Mill Communities* (Presbyterian College Press, 1943).

15. Marjorie H. Potwin, *Cotton Mill People of the Piedmont* (Columbia U Press, 1927).

16. Thomas Stark, *Damned Up-Countryman: William*

Watts Ball (Duke U Press, 1969). Biography of conservative journalist who spent a long life in South Carolina,
edited two leading newspapers (*The State* and *The News &
Courier*), knew nearly all persons and -politicians of conse-
quence, and had barbed opinions of most of them.

17. V. O. Key, Jr., *Southern Politics* (Knopf, 1949; Reprint: Peter Smith, 1969; Paperback: Vintage, 1949). One
of the definitive books on the modern South. Chap. 7 deals
with S. C. politics, 20th century.

18. William D. Workman, Jr., *Case for the South* (Devin,
1960; Reprint, 1969). A conservative's view on race relations.

Section D: STUDIES OF ATTITUDES AND CHARACTERISTICS

Two twentieth-century books about the South demonstrate
a great deal of insight into the attitudes and mores of the
region. Both are sympathetic with the South, Southerners,
and their problems; both are by Carolinians:

1. W. J. Cash, *The Mind of the South* (Knopf, 1941;
Paperbacks: Doubleday Anchor, 1954; Vintage, 1961). One
of the classics of Southern historiography, by a journalist
(*Charlotte News*) who grew up in the Blacksburg-Shelby
area, began college at Wofford, and moved on to Wake
Forest. As frequently cited as almost any book; it is a
romantic interpretation of history. It is as valuable now for
the contrast evident to the modern reader as he is struck
by the changes in the South since the book was written, as
it is for its content.

2. James McBride Dabbs, *Southern Heritage* (Knopf,
1958). A native of Sumter County, this former English professor at Coker and elsewhere has a knack for provocative
and penetrating observations on the South. Viewed as a
liberal on race relations by those who are conservative on
them, this moderate is sympathetic with his native region as
it copes with its problems. Like Cash, his prose is almost
haunting in its charm that at times approaches poetry.

XXI

Recent Developments

Obviously, this topic still rests largely among newspaper clippings. A few titles are listed below as proof that "contemporary history is reaching more permanent form and receiving re-examination. Several revolutions have been taking place in South Carolina since 1940—a new industrial revolution, drastic economic changes, social overhaul, educational renaissance (or much talk of one), development of a two-party system, and many other things.

The general histories of the South (listed in Chapter 20) have chapters on this transformation, and dramatic statistics which underscore the changes under way. Thomas D. Clark, *Emerging South* (Oxford U Press, 1961; Rev. ed., 1968; Paperback, 1968) is a general study of the region since 1920. To a degree, perhaps Southern history began as a separate entity with its own flavor and story about 1820 and ended in the 1920's as the region merged back into the history of the nation. The problems, the developments, the attitudes, and even the appearances are not so unique as to merit a separate story quite so much as they once were. The A & P in Summerville is much like the A & P in Seattle; the Texaco station in Kingstree resembles a Texaco station in Kalamazoo; the decision about a downtown mall in Rock Hill raises the same questions as it does in Rock Island. Even racial tensions are by no means a monopoly of the South, and perhaps even yet the South will find suitable solutions for these before other regions will—as a number of Southern moderates have long been saying.

A few biographies provide some information on recent history: W. D. Workman, Jr., *The Bishop from Barnwell* (R. L. Bryan, 1963), on Edgar Brown; John K. Cauthen, *Speaker Blatt* (R. L. Bryan, 1965), on Sol Blatt; and James F. Byrnes, *All in One Lifetime* (Harper & Row, 1958), an autobiography. But most politicians will have to wait. Olin Johnston and Strom Thurmond have been written about—but more by hero-worshipers than by biographers.

Maybe the best way to look at recent developments in South Carolina is to read some of the new studies of the South as a whole. A listing of what already exists could be voluminous, but a few samples are suggested:

1. George A. Buchanan, "Xenophobia in the South," in S. C. Hist. Assoc. *Procdgs.*, 1947, pp. 21–35.

2. Ralph McGill, "The South Has Many Faces," in *Atlantic*, CCXI (April, 1963), 83–98.

3. James McBride Dabbs, *Who Speaks for the South?* (Funk & Wagnalls, 1964; Paperback). Another of Dabbs' books that comes closer to having "its finger on the pulse of the South" than do most studies.

4. Harry Ashmore, *Epitaph for Dixie* (Norton, 1958). Ashmore, native of Greenville, began his journalism career in his native city. His notable career in some ways has paralleled that of W. J. Cash, and this book seeks to be the sequel—the updating—of *The Mind of the South*.

5. Fletcher M. Green, "Resurgent Southern Sectionalism, 1933–1955," in *N. C. Hist. Rev.*, XXXIII (April, 1956), 222–40.

6. George B. Tindall, "The Benighted South: Origins of a Modern Image," in *Va. Qtrly. Rev.*, XL (Spring, 1964), 281–94.

7. Willie Morris (ed.), *South Today: 100 Years After Appomattox* (Harper & Row, 1965; Paperback). Collection

of essays, mostly by Southerners, seeking to draw "a useful portrait of the present-day South."

8. Robert Sherrill, *Gothic Politics in the Deep South* (Grossman, 1968; Paperback: Ballentine, 1969). A look at the careers of a number of Southern politicians and the Southern scene. Chap. 8 deals with Bob Jones University; chap. 9, with Strom Thurmond.

There are a few surveys of the recent Southern scene in general. Good is William T. Polk, *Southern Accent* (Morrow, 1953). A bit later is Avery Leiserson (ed.), *American South in the 1960's* (Praeger, 1964; Paperback). Our transformations are chronicled in Allan P. Sindler (ed.), *Change in the Contemporary South* (Duke U Press, 1963). A good psychoanalysis is Henry Savage (of Camden), *Seeds of Time: Background of Southern Thinking* (Holt, 1959). Most entertaining is a look at the charms of that most influential Southern institution, the country store—Thomas D. Clark, *Pills, Petticoats, and Plows* (Bobbs-Merrill, 1944; Reprint: U of Okla Press, 1964), for which some of the research was done in South Carolina rural emporiums. Clark has another wistful, at times humorous one: *The Rural Press and the New South* (LSU Press, 1948). A growing institution in the New South is treated by F. R. Marshall in his *Labor in the South* (Harvard U Press, 1967), a study of labor unions. The church is getting much attention—of more than one kind; two recent books on this subject are Samuel Hill, *Southern Churches in Crisis* (Holt, Rinehart and Winston, 1967; Paperback: Beacon Press, 1968), and Kenneth Bailey, *Southern White Protestantism in the Twentieth Century* (Harper & Row, 1964).

CONSCIOUS OMISSIONS

The compiler has intentionally omitted three quite significant types of historical writing on South Carolina topics: (1) local histories, (2) histories of institutions, and (3) biographies. The omission can be justified both by lack of space and the ease with which one can locate what he seeks among these.

1. A list of county and town histories would take many pages. Some of these books were carefully done and are admirable works; others leave much to be desired. Many of them quickly become rather scarce, and hence one can quickly learn from any library card catalog just how frustrated he may be. The best collection of them to be found in the state is probably at the South Caroliniana Library in Columbia—as is true of anything dealing with the history of the Palmetto State.

2. The same generalization can be made about histories of schools and colleges, religious denominations, individual churches, and even business organizations or corporations. Many exist, and one can easily find out whether there is one about the institution in which he is interested. Several of the college histories are quite excellent pieces of scholarship and contribute much to the history of the state. The church histories usually are disappointing—particularly in view of the fact that so many South Carolinians have been church-related. Too often these histories look inward rather than seek to tie the church to the society and community of which it is a part. Granted, it may be difficult to judge how much impact religion has actually had on society, but it should be a challenge to some historian—and certainly a most awesome challenge for churchmen.

3. Biographies of South Carolinians are numerous—especially for the antebellum era. A few have been listed here, but in general they have been omitted. Bibliographies and footnotes in books will point the way to most of them, and the reader again can easily learn whether his library has biographies of the Carolina personalities in whom he is interested. He should beware of the pitfalls since so many biographers fall in love with their subjects and hence lose their critical facility. If one approaches Calhoun, for ex-

ample, he would do well to consult reviews of the biographies available before he picks the one with the prettiest
binding and concludes that he has the gospel on the subject.
He always would do well to know whether the biographer
was a nephew or grandson of the subject; there are such in
abundance in South Carolina historiography.

EPILOGUE

The compiler of this little booklet saw his task as being
simply to stand in the road and there to point at some of
the paths. Now, go thou and read. Teach thyself the history
of the Palmetto state.

Tricentennial Studies, Number 1

The Promised Land

The History of the South Carolina Land Commission, 1869–1890

Carol K. Rothrock Bleser

During the Reconstruction, the State of South Carolina began a unique program to provide freedmen with an opportunity to become landowners. As land was the principal form of wealth in the South, owning property was probably the only effective means by which freedmen could have achieved lasting economic equality.

Dr. Bleser has used important primary materials rediscovered in the South Carolina Archives in 1961 to write this definitive study of an almost forgotten social experiment, the South Carolina Land Commission. Although it is apparent that the concept of Negro landownership sponsored by a single state was far ahead of the public thinking of the age, the Promised Land Community gives us a glimpse of what might have been.

"The author is to be congratulated on a discerning use of many primary materials only recently discovered. She has managed to weave the story of the Land Commission into a wide outline of the history of Reconstruction in South Carolina in a demonstration of craftsmanship.

"*The Promised Land* is the first volume of the Tricentennial Studies series, . . . and her work is a good omen of what may be expected from this ambitious historical project of South Carolina."

—*The North Carolina Historical Review*

xvi / 190 pages   LC 78-79127 ISBN 0-87249-148-X $6.95

University of South Carolina Press
Columbia, South Carolina 29208

South Carolina Classics

Red Hills and Cotton: An Upcountry Memory
BY BEN ROBERTSON

". . . one finds an amazing timelessness, a perennially moving quality in Robertson's testament of love for his land and his people. . . . *Red Hills and Cotton* is a moving experience for the reader. . . ."

—*Atlanta Journal* and *Atlanta Constitution*

". . . as delightful a book as I remember. It is a book I have tried to keep, but my enthusiasm for it has caused me to lend it frequently, and sooner or later it wouldn't come back. That meant I'd have to get another. . . . I have made a firm resolution not to lend it anymore."

—*Chattanooga Times*

A Dutch Fork Farm Boy
BY JAMES M. ELEAZER

"His work has simplicity, complete honesty, and earthy charm. . . . It is a real contribution to one segment of America. . . ."

—*Progressive Farmer*

"[Eleazer] differs from the common run of us, however, in his ability to write simply, charmingly and vividly of the times that used to be. His book is a delightful account of everyday things that all too often are unrecorded but which are as truly a part of history as are the fighting of battles and the doings of bigwigs."

—*Jackson Sun*